Restoring Hope in America

◆

The Social Security Solution

Sam Beard

ICS PRESS
Institute for Contemporary Studies
San Francisco, California

HD
7125
B35
1996

This book is a publication of the Institute for Contemporary Studies, a nonpartisan, nonprofit, public policy research organization. The analyses, conclusions, and opinions expressed in ICS Press publications are those of the authors and not necessarily those of the Institute or of its officers, its directors, or others associated with, or funding, its work.

Inquiries, book orders, and catalog requests should be addressed to ICS Press, 720 Market Street, San Francisco, CA 94102. (415) 981-5353. Fax (415) 986-4878. For book orders and catalog requests, call toll free in the United States: (800) 326-0263.

Cover design by Ben Santora. Interior design by Herman & Company. Line illustrations by Jack Jurden. Photography by the author. Special editorial services by Farah and Associates. Book set in Berkeley Old Style Book and Bauer Bodoni type by ExecuStaff and printed and bound by Haddon Craftsmen, Inc., an RR Donnelley & Sons Company.

0 9 8 7 6 5 4 3 2 1

Library of Congress Cataloging-in-Publication Data

Beard, Sam, 1939–
    Restoring hope in America: the Social Security solution / Sam Beard.
        p.   cm.
    Includes bibliographical references
    ISBN 1-55815-489-2 (paper)
    1. Retirement income—United States.   2. Social security—United States.   3. Old   age   pensions—United   States.
    4. Finance, Personal—United States.   I. Title.
    HD7125.B35 1996
    332.024'01—dc20   95-22779
                                                              CIP

Contents

Foreword

This is a book about your future. It boldly argues that you can help to create a better economic future for all Americans by joining together with your fellow citizens to seek uniquely American solutions to our common problems. Its message is one of hope and opportunity.

This book is for every American, because it bears on our character as a people. Since our founding we have been a hopeful and optimistic nation. Yet today many of us seriously question whether there is much to look forward to. A creeping cynicism has begun to show at the fringes of our once optimistic and can-do culture. Sam Beard has decided that this state of affairs is unacceptable. In typical American style, he wants to start talking about it—to open a discussion with you on ways to give all our citizens a real stake in a growing and prosperous America.

At the heart of this discussion is an issue that affects each of us every day and has a profound impact on our economic opportunities: Social Security. As you probably suspect, our Social Security system is headed for bankruptcy. But politicians never want to be the bearers of bad news, so they avoid telling us this truth. The reality is that the system created more than sixty years ago is broken, and it has to be fixed. You have to understand only one set of facts to see why the system must be reformed. In 1945, 20 American workers supported one person on Social Security (and Medicare did not exist). Today 3.1 Americans support one person on Social Security and Medicare. By 2030 that number will be lower than 2 Americans to support each beneficiary.

It is little wonder that today young Americans have no confidence that they will ever receive benefits from Social Security. This disbelief underlies the cynicism and distrust that we all increasingly feel toward government and particularly Social Security. As a country, we simply must have retirement systems that can do their job in the complex future toward which we are rapidly accelerating. Our private pension system needs an overhaul, too; and Beard suggests what needs to be done to it. But by far the more urgent need is to revamp Social Security.

So what can we do? Should we continue the worrisome pattern of complaining and being passive victims, or should we take action for a better future? Sam Beard is taking action. Long concerned about creating economic opportunity and fairness for all Americans, the author started out to write a wide-ranging book on this subject. He soon saw, however, that reforming Social Security was not only important but fundamental to improving the way we Americans create economic opportunity. His primary question has been, Can we create a country of savers and give every American a stake in a Social Security system that allows individuals to own their accounts and that puts a good part of our contributions to work in the private sector to create more jobs and more wealth? The answer is an unqualified yes!

Beard has created a workable alternative to our failing Social Security system. By demonstrating that there are options, he has also taken the first, necessary step to restoring hope in America. Beard's plan for reforming Social Security is based in part on systems that are already working elsewhere in the world. Yet he has done more by outlining a uniquely American system. In developing his proposal, Beard has listened to what Americans want. By talking with scores of working Americans he has been able to build a reform model that takes into account the frustrations and dreams of real people. Beard's research has clearly shown that Americans are still committed to the idea of Social Security as a safety net that will be there for all of us. Yet Americans also want to have much greater control than they now do over their contributions to Social Security—they want an account with their name on it. They also want to be able to pass their retirement nest egg on to their children, and they want safeguards so that politicians in Washington will not be able to spend their money.

How should we proceed now? The recent—and shameful—Medicare debate in Washington gives us a clear example of what we should *not* do. Washington simply is not the place to start discussing how we Americans want to reform Social Security. The paramount purpose of this book, therefore, is to start a national debate on how to reform Social Security so that all Americans will have a real stake in the system. Beard's Social Security plan will work—but so may some other system not yet devised. Rather, this book provides a starting point from which to launch this discussion.

What can *you* do? If you want a better future for yourself and your children you must become involved in this national discussion. All of us, together, must build a national consensus on what we really want. Only when we have built this consensus will our representatives in Washington follow our lead and reform Social Security as a growth and opportunity program for all Americans.

A real debate on reform requires us to understand that the old political categories are no longer of any value. As I have watched Beard develop this book and have myself talked with many Americans about it, I have found that the words *conservative* or *liberal*, *Republican* or *Democrat* have very little meaning. We must also understand that any workable alternative will have both private and public components. The only question will concern how we govern a new system built on such a mix of private and public enterprise. I believe that citizens of all political dispositions are ready to come together to reform Social Security and guarantee all Americans a stake in a new system. Sam Beard, ICS Press, and I hope that you will join us in this important endeavor. For all of us together to reflect and choose a new economic future based on hope and opportunity will rebuild our confidence in ourselves, restoring American self-reliance to its rightful place in our national character.

Robert B. Hawkins, Jr.
President
Institute for Contemporary Studies

Acknowledgments

The most important thanks for making *Restoring Hope in America* a reality go to Bob Hawkins, my publisher. We met fortuitously, knowing nothing of each other's professional background. As we talked, we discovered a shared interest in crafting reforms that would expand economic opportunity in America; and he encouraged me to write a book that ICS Press could consider for publication. Until then I hadn't known that, as president of the Institute for Contemporary Studies, he directs the Press. Bob is a man of vision, an enthusiast for constitutional democracy, and a devotee of effective public policy. To him, my special thanks.

Next, I am grateful to my brother, Anson, a Wall Street investment banker, and to Adam Meyerson, editor of the Heritage Foundation's *Policy Review*. Both were instrumental in setting me on a course of "running the numbers" to prove that Americans can afford the transition from a pay-as-you-go Social Security system to a funded system.

The 1994–1995 Bipartisan Commission on Entitlement and Tax Reform played an important role in the direction of the book. Under the courageous leadership of Senator J. Robert Kerrey (Democrat of Nebraska) and Senator John C. Danforth (Republican of Missouri), the Entitlement Commission has played a vital role in dramatizing that the nation is on a perilous course—spending beyond its means and threatening our very future. Fred Goldberg, the commission's executive director, and Mark Weinberger, chief of staff, have been especially helpful to me.

Equal acknowledgment is due the 1994–1995 Advisory Council on Social Security. David C. Lindeman, the executive director of the council, has been particularly kind to me and has helped guide me into the complicated world of Social Security analysis: the laws, the relevant government documents, and how to use the data. Dave is a very knowledgeable, top professional with a generous spirit.

Conducting a financial analysis of Social Security and the transition to a funded system has been, to say the least, complicated and demanding. In the nation only a handful of top experts really stand out in their knowledge of the numbers involved. Many of these men and women spent countless hours of their time with me, and were exceptionally encouraging. They guided me again and again, and were remarkably patient. This group includes Stephen C. Goss, Stephen J. Entin, Aldona and Gary Robbins, Sylvester Schieber, and Bruce D. Schobel.

Two individuals were exceptional in helping me draft the text and organize the material: Patricia Beard and Breck England, who specialize in effective writing and whose professionalism and kind assistance were invaluable. Joseph Farah added valuable final touches to enhance the text.

In addition, many friends and colleagues read the manuscript, reread it, and guided me throughout the many months of writing. Burt Tauber stands out for being amazingly encouraging and helpful throughout a three-year period. Others whose recommendations were incorporated time and again are Jody Ambrosino, Nancy Blumberg, Lee Carter, Ernie Dannemann, Tony DeLuca, Wendell Fenton, Tom Graves, Roger Horchow, Glenn Kenton, Don Kirtley, Barry Lemieux, Shannon Leonard, Michael McCudden, Sam Shipley, Howard Simon, David and Elaine Singleton, Richard Stokes, Lee Tashijian, John Westergaard, and Paul Weatherly.

Throughout the research and writing process, I was fortunate to receive guidance from many of the nation's leading policy experts, individuals who have spent their whole professional lives dealing with pensions, Social Security, finance, and entitlements. These experts, who have reached the top of their fields and were always there to help and advise me, include Lea Abdnor, David George Ball, Theodore Benna, Peter Bourne, Barry Bosworth, John Duncan, Pete du Pont, Bob Embry, Jeff Faux, Karen Ferguson, Peter Ferrara, John Fund, Michael Gordon, Donald Grubbs, Randy Hardock, Paul Hewitt, Neil Howe, Richard Jackson, Edwin Johnson, Mary King, Laurence Kotlikoff, Ed Lopez, William Lessard, Will Marshall, Meredith Miller, Richard Rahn, John Rother, Dallas Salisbury, Ray Schmitt, Eugene Steuerle, Michael Tanner, Richard Thau, Norman Ture, Michelle Varnhagen, Carolyn Weaver, Tom Woodruff, and Mary Jane Yarrington.

In any project this absorbing, family support is essential. My wife, Joan, has been most understanding. When I disappeared at all hours in the morning, late at night, or on weekends, she remained supportive and unflustered. Alex and Hillary, my son and daughter, read the text and helped with the ideas, as did my in-laws—Paul and Mary Tigani, and Jeff and Nina Tigani. My five-year-old daughter, Morgan, helped by getting me to play and letting me be her horsey—to take my mind off the book.

My coworkers in the office have been amazing with research, ideas, editing, graphic design, and word processing. Over three years and thousands of hours, their enthusiasm kept spurring me on: Nancy Leonard, Kevin Sclesky, Ann Sheppard-Visali, and Linda Whitmarsh—and, toward the close of the project, Mike Hyland.

At the National Development Council, I have had the privilege of working with Bob Davenport, the president, and Barry Lang, our senior director, for close to twenty years. Together, we have tried to make a difference in public policy. This book could not have been possible without their encouragement or without the help of everyone at NDC—especially John Linner, who helped me with numerical analysis.

Highlights of the book are the topical drawings and graphic illustrations. The drawings were created by Jack Jurden, the cartoonist for the *News Journal* in Wilmington, Delaware, and past president of the Association of American Editorial Cartoonists. Timothy Barnekov and Kevin Sclesky, as well as Keith Duncan, toiled many hours trying to reduce central ideas to easy-to-understand figures.

Certainly not least, I remain indebted to the highly professional staff at ICS Press. Tracy Clagett has been a hard but dedicated taskmaster through the process of editing the text and clarifying the book's multitude of details. Kevin Heverin has shown himself a master at preparing the way for wide public acceptance of the book and its ideas.

Finally, important as it has been for me, writing the book is just the first step in bringing about reform. As the book is being published, I am working with a group of supporters to organize a national campaign to implement the kind of change I call for in these pages. Carl Wagner has been amazing in his input and ideas. Carl is one of America's most creative individuals, and thinks on a large scale. His guidance is deeply appreciated. Carl is joined by Bob Hawkins and by Bruce Chapman, the founder of Discovery Institute in Seattle.

As I continue to reach across the country, the number of people joining the effort is growing rapidly. Because this book must go to press, the list can never be complete here. But early participants include Polly Agee; J. D. Alexander; Burke Archer; Richard Baehr; Charles Bartlett; Jerry Berlin; Robert Bernhard; Leonard Bickwit, Jr.; Stuart Bilton; Michael Birch; William Block; Mary Pat Bonner; Randy Brown; Sandra Butler; Peter Cannell; Tom Cantrell; Joe Carbonell; Ned and Carroll Carpenter;

Russell Carson; Ray Chambers; David Coffrin; Richard Collins; John Craig; David Davenport; George deMan; Susan Doner; Dick Douglas; Sheila Ffolliott; Joel Fleishman; Brad Freeman; Richard Friedman; Joseph Galli, Jr.; Bill Gillespie; Howard Glicken; Elliott Golinkoff; Ed Goodman; Elizabeth Gutner; Lee Hanley; Dorcas Hardy; Warner Henry; Doug Hertz; Gary Hindes; Jim Hoge; Timothy Johnson; John Jolly; Richard Katz; Christopher Keating; Henry King; Michael Korby; Victor Kovner; Arthur Krieger; Clint Laird; Celinda Lake; Heather Lamm; Norman Lockman; Jim Martin; Joel Massel; Jerry Milbank; Darrell Minott; Anne Morrison; James Munn; Stan Nabi; Pat O'Connor; Donaldson Pillsbury; Jack Porter; Jill Pupa; Phil Reese; Dean Riesen; Edmond Reggie; Nate Shapiro; Bob Shrum; Bill Speakman; Jim Stack; Fred Steeper; Jack Stoltz; David Swayze; John Taylor; Victor Weber; Leon Weiner; John Westergaard; Douglas Wolf; John Zenko; and Peter Zurkow. I can never adequately express my appreciation to these people, or to the many others who will contribute to this effort in the future.

INTRODUCTION

Time for a Declaration
of Financial Independence

The message of this book cuts to the heart of a new revolution sweeping across America. The message addresses a concern you probably feel in your gut as intensely as I do—a helplessness and insecurity about our nation's future. It's a sentiment many of us are trying to communicate to our friends, family members, and politicians.

Americans are worried about their country's direction, and their political opinions are volatile. For proof, we need only examine the results of recent national elections. We simply don't like the way things are going. We are looking for new answers, and we are prepared to sweep out old ways for those that work. We desperately want to believe that our actions make a difference. We want to know that we still control our own destiny.

When we believe we have job security, the ability to get ahead, and that the safety and educational opportunities of our children are assured, Americans feel their country is on the right track. But these issues are among our most serious concerns today. We are fed up with the direction in which our government is leading us. We are angry and very distrustful of our politicians. Americans in both parties—liberals and conservatives—have the same concern: We are paying too much in taxes, getting too little in return, and recklessly mortgaging our future. People simply don't trust government solutions or our political leaders. Thus, a new revolution is underway—redefining the role of government as it affects people's lives and pocketbooks.

MILLIONS OF AMERICANS ARE ANGRY AND FRUSTRATED

Many of us are afraid that future opportunity is diminishing. When I interviewed people for this book, I asked, "Will your children have a higher standard of living and greater opportunities than you?" Eight out of ten immediately responded no—indicating they strongly believed their children would have a *lower* standard of living and *less* opportunity. This runs contrary to traditional American optimism. We pride ourselves in working hard, and passing expanded opportunities on to our children. America historically sees itself as a land of progress and dreams. But, a majority of Americans today feel we are on a treadmill. We are angry. And we are ready for change.

MILLIONS OF AMERICANS DISTRUST GOVERNMENT

Taxes keep going up, and more of us are recognizing there is no connection between bigger government and an improved lifestyle. Social Security is a perfect example of how the connectors between individual and government perspectives are breaking down.

It makes us angry when we learn that the government is taking our tax dollars out of the Social Security Trust Fund to pay other federal debts. People instinctively know that this is stealing—that they would be sent to jail for a similar act—and that the stockpiling of IOUs in the trust fund is fiscally unsound.

The government sees Social Security as a "manageable" problem. The government says Social Security can still be fundamentally sound if only it raises taxes two to four percentage points and cuts benefits 10 to 15 percent. Borrowing Social Security surpluses is seen as acceptable

> **To preserve our independence,** we must not let our rulers load us with perpetual debt. We must make our election between economy and liberty or profusion and servitude.
>
> —Thomas Jefferson
>
> *Source: Quoted in Concord Coalition,* The Zero Deficit Plan: A Plan for Eliminating the Federal Budget Deficit by the Year 2000 *(Washington, D.C., 1994).*

financial management. But more and more we feel abused when government forces us to pay 12.4 percent of our hard-earned money into Social Security, for someone we don't know and never will know—especially when we don't believe Social Security will be there for us when *we* retire.

We Americans know that we are in trouble as a nation. We are worried about our jobs and our standard of living. We are afraid we are harming our children's chances. It's common sense: every American knows that government overspending cannot continue indefinitely or ultimately succeed. Politicians are caught in a desperate cross-current. Change can only come from the people—from the grassroots.

People understand the meaning and power of achieving financial security. The goal is a major motivating force. It connects family, education, hard work, and savings where they should be—within the grasp of each American—not in the hands of a Washington bureaucrat or distant decision-maker. The focus is personal and local. The answers are not to be found in the nation's capital. But over the past sixty years we have built into our institutions the expectation that Washington will be a source of money, and the deliverer of services.

It's time for a change. It's time to stop relying on government for handouts. It's time to break the bonds of dependence on Washington. Americans don't have to settle for the survival wages of an antiquated Social Security system. There's a better way. We are a prosperous, industrious nation, and we are capable of instituting a plan that can—quite literally—turn every hard-working American into a millionaire. This book sets forth that plan.

A radically redesigned Social Security system can be the beginning of an economic revolution, making America's third century the era of investment, savings, and unprecedented prosperity. How? By the year 2000, more than 100 million Americans will be earning $10,000 per year or more. Allow them to set aside their Social Security payments into personal investment and retirement accounts—and they will become millionaires.

This single act will be a major step away from being *in dependence* on the government, and toward a renewed freedom and *independence* for all Americans. That's what the plan described in this book is all about—a manifesto for financial independence and security for every hard-working American. It may not contain all the answers. It may not be the ultimate solution. But it should serve as the starting place for a national debate on how to save Social Security and redirect American economic policy.

A LITTLE HISTORICAL BACKGROUND

At the birth of the nation, free opportunity to participate in our economy—a chance for a stake—was as important to individual liberty as was freedom in government. The belief in each individual's value and ability was the cornerstone of liberty and life in America. Economic opportunity and participatory government complemented each other. If weighed on a scale, economic freedom might even have outweighed political freedom in the eyes of most immigrants.

Over the years "government of the people, by the people, and for the people" has remained in the forefront of our image of ourselves; the concept is taught in every civics class and reinforced by the media.

When we think of the Founding Fathers, we can name many political heroes: the Pilgrims who landed at Plymouth, Thomas Jefferson, George Washington, Paul Revere, Alexander Hamilton, Patrick Henry, James Madison, Ben Franklin, Sam and John Adams. Each name evokes pictures of events and elicits time-tested quotations once dutifully memorized by every elementary school student: "Give me liberty or give me death." "Life, liberty and the pursuit of happiness." The lessons of each underscore our belief in political freedom and in our democratic form of government.

But where are the images of our *economic* heroes? Who are they? What have they said? Why doesn't our school system give equal emphasis to the basics of our economic freedom?

The most famous document defining America's quest for political freedom is Thomas Jefferson's Declaration of Independence. The most famous document defining our individual quest for economic freedom is Adam Smith's *Wealth of Nations*. They were both written in 1776, and they were complementary parts of a new political philosophy based on the rights of individuals to reach their full potential. Every American knows the date of the Declaration of Independence and its political impact. Probably fewer than one in a hundred know the date of *The Wealth of Nations*, and few even know what it's about.

Remember the Boston Tea Party, however. "No taxation without representation" was one of the fundamental demands of the colonists.

Now, with 275 million citizens and enormous governmental super-structures, individual Americans once again feel that their economic power is limited. They feel that they are on a treadmill. They feel that their purchasing power is stagnant, or even declining. They see taxes rising and government getting bigger. They feel that economic opportunity is slipping through their fingers—not to mention the opportunity of their children.

This was not the intention of the Founding Fathers. To them "liberty" meant that each of us has the right to a long list of freedoms: political, personal, social— and economic. When the First Continental Congress met in October 1774, the Bill of Rights it approved declared that each citizen was entitled to life, liberty, and property. In May 1776 the Second Continental Congress stated that colonists had natural rights to protect their "lives, liberties and properties."

Thomas Jefferson broke new ground in the Declaration of Independence. While the pamphleteers of the day repeated "life, liberty and property," Jefferson elevated the dialogue to a higher plateau by changing the promise to "life, liberty and the pursuit of happiness." Jefferson's phrase "the pursuit of happiness" clearly was meant to encompass the opportunity to own property and to enjoy the fruits of one's labor.

The central core of these ideas reflects the American optimism about each individual. "Government by the people" tells the world that we have faith in all Americans, their ideas, and their common sense. This same founding faith in the individual, the same belief in the worth of each person's thoughts, creativity, and ability to make a contribution to society has been the source of America's prosperity. Our economic system is based on the conviction that each of us must be allowed to pursue his or her dreams in a free marketplace. Citizens, not government, should run the economy. The sum of our unfettered dreams is the greatest opportunity for all.

But somehow we have lost our focus on the underlying economic strength of our country. Stop for a moment and think about the importance of our economy. Imagine how your life would change if America became a fourth-rate economic nation. We could all still vote, but most of us would be poor. Assuredly we would feel that the "pursuit of happiness" had slipped through our fingers. It is important to realize that among nations political power flows directly from economic power. Any country that loses its productivity and economic base loses world power. There is no necessary correlation between the *desire* to be powerful and *being* powerful.

The most important building block of American strength—the source of our wealth—is the spirit of individuals working together freely in communities. The simple dream of all immigrants, regardless of family background or origin, is that America will enable them to improve their lot through hard work and creativity. Economic opportunity for all and the chance for a stake have been the driving forces that built America into its premier world position. This heritage and these dreams remain alive today.

Success in today's economy requires innovation, risk taking, commitment to education, and hard work. Think about it: qualities needed to succeed are *American* qualities, qualities that have made us the envy of the world. Americans created a new order by believing that each individual is unique and has unique talents and abilities. These beliefs launched millions of dreams. Those dreams created energy and unparalleled success. The only nations, or group of nations, that can surpass America are those that follow our traditions and leadership better than we ourselves do.

As we look ahead, instead of settling for a future in which we are increasingly hampered and hemmed in by narrowing economic opportunities, Americans can start a new economic revolution, providing unprecedented growth and opportunity.

We need to affirm our new Declaration of Financial Independence. Starting now, we can lay the groundwork for the next stage of American opportunity through basic changes in Social Security, the pension system, and inheritance laws. If we increase the possibility of economic ownership for all, and allow all of us to be shareholders in a brighter future, before the end of our third century, America will be the land of 100 million millionaires.

The Declaration of Financial Independence

When in the course of human events, it becomes necessary for one people to break down the barriers to economic freedom and financial independence placed in their path by government, a decent respect for the rights and responsibilities of individuals and families impels them to remove the shackles of bureaucratic control. Thus, here is a plan to address the fact that in America today capital ownership is concentrated at the top. We hold this truth to be self-evident, that all Americans should have an equal opportunity to become capital owners.

Become a Millionaire through Social Security and the Pension System

1. Set aside $30 a week — $1,560 a year—tax-free.
   - After thirty years, you will have **$318,445.**
   - After forty years, you will have **$822,604.**
   - After forty-five to fifty years, you will have over **$1 million.**
   - You can begin at any age.
   - Begin setting **$25** to **$30** aside when you enter the workforce (age twenty). By age sixty-five to seventy, when you retire, you will be a millionaire.

2. Achieve economic security for your senior years.
   - Americans now live an extra fifteen to twenty years after retirement.
   - A **$1 million** pension could generate sufficient income to make your senior years truly "golden."

3. Provide a better standard of living for your children.
   - Pass your capital assets on to your children, tax-free, and their earned income can be supplemented by earnings from capital.

4. Establish two sources of income.
   - Over **100 million** Americans are in the workforce and receive payment for labor. This is the first source of income.
   - The second source of income is capital, which generates income from dividends, interest, or equity growth.

5. Democratize capital ownership.
   - When it's time to pay the country's bills, all Americans are included. Each of us pays his or her fair share of the tax burden.
   - Through Social Security and the pension system all Americans can have the opportunity to be substantial capital owners. We democratize the burden; let's democratize the rewards.

6. Make America strong.
   - Pursuing our individual economic self-interest, we can join together to help America compete in the new world economy.
   - No nation can equal our strength if we cut all Americans in on equal economic opportunity.
   - Fulfill the promise of the Founding Fathers for life, liberty, and property.

BUILDING SECURITY
FOR WORKING
AMERICANS

Life, Liberty, and Property

From the beginning, one of the major promises of America was economic opportunity. As mentioned previously, early drafts of the Declaration of Independence cited the unalienable rights of "Life, Liberty and Property." Compared with most other nations of the world, America remains a bastion of economic opportunity. Yet, at the end of the twentieth century, the top 1 percent of Americans owns 43 percent of the nation's wealth (excluding home ownership); the bottom 90 percent owns just 23 percent of the wealth.

It doesn't seem right that so many Americans are on an economic treadmill. Hard-working middle-class Americans—one- and two-income families, as well as those with lower skills working two shifts, still hovering at the poverty level—ought to have the chance to attain some measure of financial independence.

The proposal for a funded Social Security system is a viable plan to open economic opportunity to *all* Americans—and save Social Security for future generations. This plan will allow working Americans to accumulate capital two ways—through a revised, funded Social Security system with personal accounts and through private and public pensions. But before it can work, two facts must be acknowledged and addressed: Social Security as it now operates is in serious danger, and pensions need to be redesigned for the modern workplace.

WHAT'S WRONG WITH SOCIAL SECURITY?

When the baby boomers begin to retire, soon after the turn of the century, *Social Security will run out of money*—unless we raise taxes or cut benefits. According to a recent study, members of the twenty-something generation believe they are more likely to see a UFO than Social Security payments. If the system isn't radically reformed, they may be right.

Today, Social Security is run on a pay-as-you-go basis. That means current employees are taxed to pay for the benefits of retirees. And by law, you have to pay these Social Security taxes; you pay half of your assessment, and your employer pays the other half.

Nearly all experts dealing with the future solvency of Social Security accept that "Present Law" promises cannot be maintained. There are real problems, and changes will have to be made. To ensure Social Security's solvency over the next seventy-five years, these experts calculate a combination of cuts in Social Security benefits equal to 10–15 percent of the current Present Law benefits along with payroll tax increases of two to four percentage points.

WHAT'S WRONG WITH THE PRIVATE PENSION SYSTEM?

You can expect to have three or four different careers and six to ten jobs in your lifetime. Because of vesting and portability practices, too often you will lose the money in your pension every time you change jobs. Besides, most small businesses offer *no* pensions; and, increasingly, big business is outsourcing employment to avoid paying pension and health benefits.

WHAT'S WRONG WITH INHERITANCE?

Under current law, when you die, after a $600,000 exemption on your total estate, the money (the principal) in your 401(k) personal pension account and individual retirement account (IRA) is taxed twice: first through estate taxes, then as income to your heirs. These tax laws undermine the goals of savings and capital formation, which are vital for our country's future.

SOLUTIONS

Social Security   Our Social Security solution must begin by keeping our promises to current retirees. The way to save the Social Security system for future beneficiaries and ensure that you will get the full benefit of the money you put in is to create a two-tier system under Social Security.

The first tier (hereafter, Tier 1) will remain pay-as-you-go. The second tier (Tier 2) will be funded. All Americans who pay $500 or more into Social Security, up to a cap of $3,000 per year, will be allowed to set monies aside into a personal investment and retirement account. On a

100 Million Millionaires

Set aside $25–$30 per week for one working lifetime—forty-five years—either in a private pension or in a funded Social Security.

scaled formula, based on differing income levels, this includes taxes you are already paying plus a voluntary savings match. In this way, we can put the proven growth rate of the private sector to work to save Social Security—and to meet future obligations.

At the end of one working lifetime, millions of participating workers will have more than $1 million in their individual retirement accounts.

How can you afford to set the money aside? Will it require paying higher taxes? No. This is money you and your employer are already paying, along with voluntary savings matches. In one working lifetime, out of tax dollars you are already paying into Social Security:

- If you earn **$4,193** per year, you can amass a capital pool of **$430,478** with **$10** per week set aside from your taxes.
- If you earn **$8,387** per year, you can amass a capital pool of **$860,956** with **$20** per week set aside from your taxes.
- If you earn **$12,580** or more per year, you can amass a capital pool of **$1,291,433** with **$30** per week set aside from your taxes.

Here's how it works:

The best case   With expected investment growth of 8 percent in your personal account, you will receive Social Security payments from the income on your accumulated savings. In millions of cases, the income from these payments will substantially outstrip likely Social Security benefit levels, and you will control a capital nest egg to pass on to your heirs.

The middle case   Your account will grow at a lower rate. Part of your Social Security will be paid from traditional Social Security taxes (this will be Tier 1). If you purchase an annuity using the capital in your Tier 2 funded account, your Social Security benefits will still surpass likely Social Security benefits.

The worst case   The government cannot guarantee growth in private sector investments. In case of poor financial management or an economic depression, through Tier 1 traditional Social Security taxes, the government *will* guarantee a decent safety net retirement income for all.

A bonus   The strength of America's economic future is closely connected to savings and investment. Currently, America's savings rates are dangerously low. But under the Tier 2 funded system, $100 billion to

$200 billion of individual savings each year will be invested, mostly in the private sector. An extra $100 billion to $200 per year can make a significant difference.

The main question posed by economic analysts then becomes: How much of the money being set aside is net new savings? If government spending rises at the same rate as individual savings, there will be no net new savings, and no new economic growth. As citizens, we need to work with government leaders to cap government spending. Then these monies *will be* net new savings and will stimulate the American economy, creating new industries and high-paying jobs. (Please see Chapter 13 for a more extensive discussion of the savings implications of the reforms I propose.)

A growing economy will result in additional tax revenues—to help reduce the federal deficit.

A second bonus In a mature funded system, as Social Security benefits are increasingly paid by the income from your capital, your payroll taxes can be reduced.

Private Pensions Changing the Social Security system could take years. But starting now, under existing pension laws, if each employee and his or her employer will set aside $25 to $30 per week in private or public pensions, millions and millions of Americans can accumulate $1 million in addition to the money they amass in their individual Social Security accounts.

For those working part-time or for less than thirty-five years, the combined assets from Social Security and pension accounts can still make them millionaires.

A pension should be part of each worker's compensation. With immediate vesting, your first payment into your pension will come with your first paycheck on every job. With portability, when you change jobs, you will take the accumulated money with you.

If you and your employer set aside a combined $25 to $30 a week from the time you are twenty until you retire at sixty-five, your pension will exceed $1 million.

Your Heirs In addition to the existing exemption, a selected amount of the money saved in pension or Social Security accounts—a suggested $500,000 per heir at today's value of money—should be allowed to pass tax-free.

HAVING A STAKE

Ironically, in a society based on capitalism, most of us know very little about money. When the majority of Americans are capital owners, however, they will have a stake in understanding the way money works. The first thing to understand is that there are two potential sources of income. One is payment for work (for most of us this means wages). The other is capital ownership; money, in other words, makes money.

As I will discuss further in Chapter 14, the democratization of wages played an important part in building our preeminence as an industrial power. When Henry Ford *doubled* the going wage in 1914 and started to pay his workers $5 a day, this event made headlines around the world and touched off an economic revolution. At the end of the century, we can start another economic revolution. Through the Social Security and pension savings plans, we can democratize capital ownership:

- More than **100 million** Americans can have a second source of income—income from capital. This will create a whole new round of economic growth.
- Extending the possibility of capital ownership to all working Americans will establish a **$50 trillion** to **$100 trillion** capital pool. No nation can begin to compete with this level of capital power.
- If we pass this money tax-free to our children, we can save their standard of living.

STARTING A NATIONAL DEBATE

The purpose of this book is to start a national debate on our values as they relate to economic opportunity and fairness in America.

We are rapidly becoming two societies. The top 25 percent of American families have high-paying jobs with bonuses and have worldwide opportunities to accumulate wealth and capital. They will thrive in the new world economy and the new information/internet age. They are on a fast track, and opportunities abound for them. But the next 75 percent of all American families earn $50,000 or less annually. They are hurting. They are on a treadmill, as we see in Chapter 4.

Let's stop and think about a family earning $50,000 or less. After paying their taxes, covering their regular living expenses, looking after their children, and meeting their home and car payments (where these exist), what is left over?

During the 1980s and into the 1990s, for the most part, their real wages have been declining. They have little or no savings. Their opportunity to participate in the rewards of a free market economy by building a nest egg or owning capital is very limited. Regardless of how hard they work, they don't feel that they control their lives or that they can pass a better opportunity on to their children.

A remodeled pension system and remodeled Social Security, designed for the twenty-first century, can restore hope for all Americans. Let's talk about it. Let's start a national debate. Let's take a fresh and bold look at our policy alternatives. This debate needs to be about:

- how our institutions can be shaped to give each of us the opportunity to become a capital owner and a shareholder in America's dreams
- acceptable levels of taxation
- how much control we want as individuals, and how much control we are willing to relinquish to the federal government

LET'S START A NATIONAL DEBATE ON ECONOMIC OPPORTUNITY AND FAIRNESS IN AMERICA

We are rapidly becoming a divided society, in which 75 percent of all American families earn $50,000 and under. Their real wages are declining. They have little or no savings. They feel that they are caught in a rut with no control over their destinies.

How can our institutions be shaped to build capital ownership so that all Americans can become shareholders in America's dreams?

♦

UNDER SOCIAL SECURITY

The first mandate is to keep our promises to existing retirees.

We need to amend the private and public pension systems so that they are consistent with the modern workplace. We need new approaches to allow individuals to build retirement nest eggs, uninterrupted throughout their working lives, even as they change jobs six to ten times.

Under Social Security we can establish important guidelines to shape the debate:

1. The first guideline is to guarantee that existing retirees receive their promised benefits.
2. The second guideline is to design a system so that all individuals are treated with decency and receive a sustainable and adequate standard of living in retirement. Americans want a standard that protects all of us as individuals with decency.
3. The third guideline is to ensure that we save Social Security. Social Security was created in 1935 and in many ways has been one of America's most successful social systems. I think citizens will agree that we need to update Social Security to ensure that it can continue to keep its promises—and even expand its benefits—in the twenty-first century.
4. The fourth guideline is to explore how Social Security can offer all Americans the opportunity to build a capital ownership stake.

A PART OF HISTORY

I have benefited from every opportunity this country has to offer, and I have experienced the best in America. At the same time, through my work in economic development, trying to create jobs and opportunity in America's urban and rural slums, I've experienced the worst in America—the debris of broken promises.

My great-grandfather was James Jerome Hill, the founder of the Great Northern Railroad and one of America's outstanding business leaders; and our family was part of America's social elite. I went to the best private schools, along with other children whose ancestors—Rockefellers, du Ponts, Fricks, and Mellons—had also been part of the great economic revolution that opened opportunity in America at the turn of this century.

Many of these makers of history, like my great-grandfather, who was born to limited means in Guelph, Upper Canada, and had little formal education, were able to succeed through hard work. They were self-made. Hill's accomplishments, beginning with nothing and building an empire, helped to shape my sense of optimism that an individual really can make a difference. He had a vision of opening the West, and built a railroad through the wilderness, from St. Paul, Minnesota, to Seattle, Washington. James J. Hill's railroad literally populated the Northwest. My great-grandfather became a major figure in American economic and social history, and he lived the American dream. If your home is in one of certain western states, you probably still celebrate James J. Hill Day.

Developing Economic Opportunity   I was born in New York City. After school, in my mid-twenties, I had the privilege of working with Senator Robert Kennedy on the restoration of Bedford-Stuyvesant, one of America's worst slums, in the heart of Brooklyn. After the senator was assassinated, I set up the National Development Council, a nonprofit corporation specializing in economic development and low-income housing. During the past twenty-five years we've worked in more than forty states and in over 130 cities, and have had the excitement of creating and then running economic development programs for Presidents Nixon, Ford, Carter, and Reagan.

After twenty-five years, the National Development Council has made possible more than $25 billion of financing, arranged financing for more than 20,000 businesses, and created more than half a million jobs. We have a small professional staff which has never exceeded thirty. Our strength is identifying powerful ideas. Then we create local partnerships and build local know-how to carry out these ideas. We've trained over 30,000 local professionals in the techniques of job creation, credit, working with banks, and selecting and financing projects.

The accomplishments of the National Development Council have been based on our dreams—a vision of what could be—a very clear sense of what is possible, and hard work. Those are the same elements that are the mainstay of this book, which presents a goal of new opportunity for all Americans and a vision of an expanding America. As I will show in succeeding chapters, we have a choice. We can pit one generation against another—the young vs. the old—and fight over a stagnated economy, or we can create 100 million shareholders in a growing America, and save the American dream for our children.

The past twenty-five years that I have spent in economic development have been an invaluable training ground preparing me to wrestle with these issues. Over the past three years, I have undertaken the necessary, intensive research to develop workable solutions to the problem of financial independence for working Americans. I have gone all across the country and interviewed economists, Social Security and pension experts, historians, politicians, and political advisers. I've read hundreds of books and articles, and turned the numbers upside down and inside out hoping to come up with an opening in the face of what seemed like an impenetrable wall.

Piece by piece, a little at a time, the interviews, research, and calculations showed the way. As long as I can remember, I've believed that part of my great-grandfather's legacy was the challenge to all of us that we have it in our power to create the energy and sense of open-ended possibility, the excitement about what America can be, and what we as Americans can do for ourselves that the opening of the West evoked a hundred years ago.

A WINDOW OF OPPORTUNITY

The most important element in what I propose is that creating 100 million millionaires is *doable*. We have a window of opportunity of five to eight years. If we wait until 2010 or 2020, the baby boomers will be retiring, and Social Security and Medicare will be running $200 billion to $300 billion annual deficits. We will no longer be able to afford to fund the personal retirement accounts that this book proposes. But if we put this system in place and create a shared vision of broad-scale ownership in America, we can save the standard of living of our children and grandchildren.

America is on a collision course with its destiny. Average citizens know that we are in trouble, and they fear for the future of our children. As America ages, the critical question is, How do we finance the support systems—Social Security and Medicare? I will establish important contrasts between the old way of financing society's needs and a new way.

Under the old way, we will have to raise taxes and cut benefits. As we continue to raise taxes, we're damaging our underlying economic strength by further reducing savings and investment—the lifeblood of our economy.

The new way, as described in this book, is based on a new vision of individual capital ownership, and will truly open economic opportunity to all Americans. But this will require changes in the way we do things. The answers, the leadership, and the power come from you. Power begins with individual ideas and individual ambition. Your dreams can create energy—and results. You and your neighbors, working side by side in your local community, can bring about the change necessary to create your own economic strength. That simple idea was the founding principle of America in 1776, and it remains equally powerful today.

With the plan outlined in these pages, we can break through the walls we all face. But the ideas are only the first step. America needs your help to implement the ideas. Change can occur only if we band together to demand a new vision. With your help, America can do what all of our ancestors did: leave behind the kind of thinking that narrowly restricts life, and set out to open new frontiers of opportunity.

Twelve Secrets They Don't Want You to Know

Th ere are reasons your government keeps secrets from you. Elected leaders and bureaucrats sometimes prefer to bury information vital to our nation's economic health and your personal financial well-being. Why do they do this?

- because the only way the federal government can keep its promises is to raise taxes
- because if you were allowed to invest your Social Security taxes in a personal account managed by private sector financial managers, you would have far more income than Social Security provides
- because to cover the depth of its financial problems, the government often uses misleading numbers and statistics

For these and other reasons, government leaders keep hundreds of secrets. Here are my top twelve—every one taken from official government reports. You can add your own.

RAISING TAXES

Secret No. 1   If Social Security benefits aren't cut, payroll taxes will need to increase more than two percentage points by 2020, more than four percentage points by 2030, and between five and six points by 2070.

Secret No. 2   The government projects that payroll taxes will be raised to 25.69 percent by 2030 to meet the expected costs for Social Security, federal disability insurance, and federal health insurance (Medicare Part A). That's *before* we will be asked to pay federal income tax and state and local taxes.

Secret No. 3   By 2030, federal expenses are projected to reach between 35 and 40 percent of GDP (gross domestic product—the total economic output within the country). To meet these obligations, *all* federal taxes will have to double from the existing 19 percent level.

THE BATTLE OF THE GENERATIONS: OLD VS. YOUNG

Secret No. 4   Under current laws, unless we change them, the old and the young in America are on the most serious, headlong collision course. To pay the full benefits baby boomers expect, young workers will have to pay unconscionably increased taxes. But if we don't raise taxes on the young generation, aging boomers will face massive cuts in Social Security and Medicare benefits. Under the old system we have, it's nobody's fault, but the old are being pitted against the young, fighting over a dwindling pie.

Without staggering tax increases on the young, the baby boomers face a 40 percent reduction in benefits. But to keep our promises to aging Americans, young workers face a 68 percent payroll tax increase and higher income taxes, all—again—before paying state and local taxes. These tax levels exceed a 60 percent lifetime tax rate.

MONEY THAT COULD BE YOURS

Secret No. 5   An individual earning $30,000 per year is paying $3,720 annually into Social Security. On retirement, if taxes are not increased, the individual will receive $13,710 per year for life from Social Security—and no capital to pass along to heirs. But if you could invest $2,500 per year in a personal investment account under Social Security, earning 8 percent per year, for one working lifetime—after forty-five years, you would have a retirement fund of $2,069,605.

Forty-five years from now, $2 million will not have the same value as it does today; but it will still be a substantial amount. Discount expected inflation, and the retirement fund would be worth $368,481

Generational Accounting: Old and Young Fight over a Dwindling Pie

By 2030 spending on the elderly and near-elderly, plus interest on the debt, will consume more than all the revenues anticipated to be available to the federal government, thus crowding out educating our youth, helping children who already have the highest poverty rates in the nation, preventing crime, restoring promise and order in our center cities, defense, our environment, and everything else.

(Source: Eugene Steuerle, coauthor of Retooling Social Security for the Twenty-first Century, *personal communication.*)

- *Individuals born in* **1900** *paid a* **24 percent** *lifetime tax rate.*
- *Individuals born in* **1970** *face a* **36 percent** *lifetime tax rate—a* **50 percent** *increase in just sixty years.*
- *Future generations face an* **82 percent** *lifetime tax rate.*

(Source: Laurence Kotlikoff, Boston University and the National Bureau of Economic Research, personal communication.)

Generational Accounting: Old and Young Join Together to Preserve the Vision of Expanded Opportunity for All

An intergenerational fight is unacceptable and unnecessary. With funded personal accounts under Social Security, older Americans can retire in comfort and pass the capital tax-free to their heirs.

in today's money. At 5 percent income, the individual would receive $18,424 per year for life. And through a change in the inheritance laws, the $2 million could be passed along tax-free.

Under the proposed system, if you chose a lifetime annuity, you could receive $29,256 a year for your expected lifetime—more than twice the regular Social Security benefit.

STOCKPILED DEBTS, MISLEADING STATISTICS, AND OUTRIGHT MISTAKES

Secret No. 6   You're paying extra taxes into the Social Security Trust Fund to create a surplus—a cushion to protect the huge number of baby boomers who will be eligible for Social Security early in the next century. By the year 2020, the fund should contain $3 trillion; but there won't be a penny there. The government is spending it all. The government tells you that you share a $3 trillion asset. But there's no real money in the fund—just IOUs. That's a debt. Payable by you! And you'll have to be taxed again—over $36,000 per family—to pay it!

Secret No. 7   The first annual deficit for Social Security is projected in 2013: $7.3 billion. This will grow to over $100 billion in 2022, grow to over $200 billion in 2032, and reach $225.1 billion per year by 2040.

In one working lifetime—forty-five years—Social Security is projected to have an accumulated debt of $4.1 trillion. This is projected to grow to $20.9 trillion by 2070—seventy-five years—the normal period to determine Social Security's long-term solvency.

The Social Security Trust Fund

You're paying extra taxes to create a surplus. The government is spending it all. There's no real money in the fund—just IOUs.

Existing Social Security

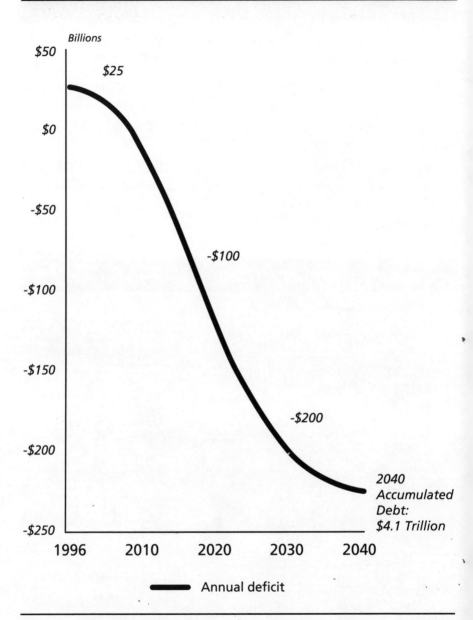

Billions

$25

2040
Accumulated
Debt:
$4.1 Trillion

────── Annual deficit

Source: Federal Old-Age and Survivors Insurance and Disability Insurance Trust Fund (OASDI),
Board of Trustees, 1994 Annual Report. House Document 103-231(Washington, D.C.: U.S.
Government Printing Office, April 12, 1994).

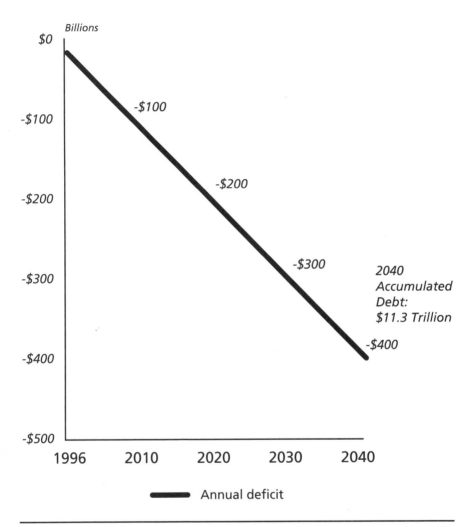

Medicare Part A (HI) (in constant 1994 dollars)

Source: Federal Old-Age and Survivors Insurance and Disability Insurance Trust Fund (OASDI), Board of Trustees, 1994 Annual Report. House Document 103-231 (Washington, D.C.: U.S. Government Printing Office, April 12, 1994).

Secret No. 8   In 1996 Medicare Part A (HI—inpatient hospital services) will run a $14 billion deficit. This will grow to over $100 billion per year in 2011, over $200 billion per year in 2022, over $300 billion per year in 2031, and over $400 billion per

Medicare Part B (SMI) (in constant 1994 dollars)

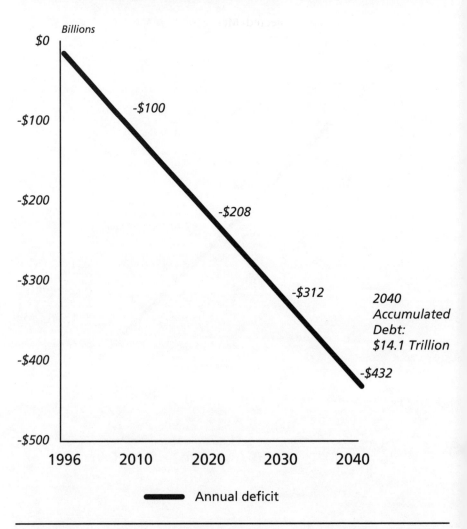

2040 Accumulated Debt: $14.1 Trillion

Annual deficit

Source: Federal Supplementary Medical Insurance Trust Fund (SMI), Board of Trustees, 1994 Annual Report, House Document 103-229 (Washington, D.C.: U.S. Government Printing Office, April 12, 1994).

year in 2040. In one working lifetime—forty-five years—Medicare Part A (HI) is projected to have an accumulated $11.3 trillion debt.

In 1996 Medicare Part B (SMI—physician's services and outpatient hospital services) will run a $4.2 billion deficit. This will grow to over

$100 billion per year in 2008, over $200 billion per year in 2017, over $300 billion per year in 2026, and over $400 billion per year in 2035. In one working lifetime—forty-five years—Medicare Part B (SMI) is projected to have an accumulated $14.1 trillion debt.

In 2040, the annual projected Medicare deficit—Part A and Part B combined—will be $835.6 billion per year. The accumulated Part A and Part B combined debt will be $25.4 trillion.

Secret No. 9   The federal government's unfunded liability for federal employees and military pensions is $1.5 trillion.

Secret No. 10   The *Economic Report of the President* hides the true annual deficit by finding ways to report lower numbers. In 1994, the *Economic Report* listed a $181 billion deficit. The true deficit was $250 billion. To make the numbers seem less dismal, the government "borrows" surpluses from Social Security and other trust funds, and stockpiles those IOUs I've mentioned before.

Secret No. 11   Politicians often understate the total national debt by as much as 33 percent. To mask the truth, the debt is reported in two separate categories: "borrowed from the people" and "borrowed from the government." In 1994, the "borrowed from the people" debt was $3.6 trillion. "Borrowed from the government" adds an additional $1.3 trillion. This means that the true national debt is $4.9 trillion.

Secret No. 12   In 1988 the Social Security Trustees' Report projected a hearty $11.8 trillion trust fund. Only six years later, in 1994, the trustees revised this projection to the $3 trillion I have cited previously. The 1988 numbers were wrong by $8.8 trillion.

In 1988, the trustees estimated that Social Security would run out of money in 2048. Only six years later, in 1994, the trustees projected that Social Security will become insolvent in 2029. The 1988 numbers were wrong by nineteen years.

Americans on a Treadmill

I f you're a typical working American, you're on the money treadmill, and you feel as if you're losing ground. You're working harder and your paycheck is buying less. You're frustrated. You're worried. You're paying taxes, but you're angry. You see so much government waste, and you think: They keep raising taxes. When is this going to stop?

This chapter describes the present economic situation of an average family—in the words of one family member—and shows what their future will be if we continue our current policies. I then offer a proposal for a new vision and a new future.

THE PRESENT

The following comments were spoken by a husband and father working to support his family in the 1990s. But in his concerns he is representative of millions of Americans—male or female.

"I was better off six years ago than I am today. I have a full-time job managing an oil terminal, and then I drive a truck at night and on weekends to make ends meet. My wife used to work full-time as a lab technician. Now she works part-time and looks after our two kids. I work sixty hours a week and up to eighty hours a week in the winter. My major sacrifice is for my kids. I want to send them to college and give them a better life than I had. I just barely finished high school and paid no attention to my studies.

"We're very active in the community with the kids—church, Girl Scouts, Cub Scouts, Little League baseball, and basketball in the winter. I'm exhausted; but they asked me to coach the Little League team, and I love it.

"I work 120 days—one-third of my year—to pay taxes to the government. And what for? People don't trust the government. People are really getting fed up. If government was a business, they'd be *out* of business. They're just ripping us off. You read about these crazy government studies. What for? Ask me. I could tell them that it's possible to get a cold in summer. Why spend $600,000 on a study?

"The S&Ls got into trouble, and we had to bail them out. Now banks are making record profits. Are they going to give us our money back? Don't they owe us something? Government regulations are just ripping us off. FCC, ICC, EPA, OSHA, EOC. Give me a break. How many government agencies are there and what do they do? They just shuffle papers, give themselves big raises, and make trouble for me.

"We take no elaborate vacations. We don't have furniture in our front room. We can't afford it yet. We run our car into the ground before we get a new one. We try to set $20 a week aside into an entertainment fund so that my wife and I can go out once in awhile—just by ourselves. But that money's never there. Our furnace broke down, and we really had to scrape to get a new one.

"A lot of our friends cut out health insurance. They couldn't afford it. They're gambling big time. They just keep their fingers crossed and hope that nothing happens.

"My budget is bad, but government is worse. I pay over $3,000 a year into Social Security. That's a lot of money. I really doubt it will be there when I retire. I have $1,100 in a savings account. That's it. I don't have a pension. Retire on my savings? That's a joke.

"We really need to do something before the system breaks down. In lots of ways, our life isn't bad. We've got it good compared to people around the world. I'm prepared to sacrifice and take my medicine if we can straighten this mess out and save it for our kids."

THE WAY WE'RE GOING

Warnings issued by the 1994–1995 Bipartisan Commission on Entitlement and Tax Reform (hereafter called the Entitlement Commission) chaired by two courageous lawmakers—Senator Robert Kerrey, a Democrat from Nebraska, and Senator John Danforth, a Republican from Missouri—best capture the way we're going.

Government Spending Out of Control

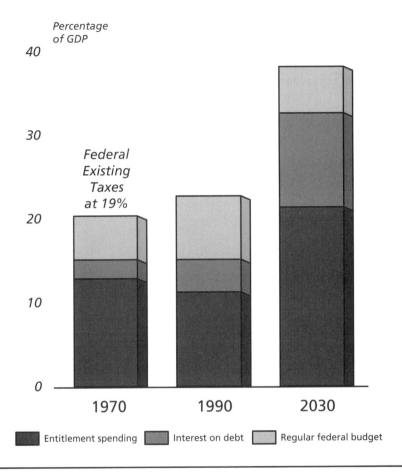

Source: Adapted from Bipartisan Commission on Entitlement and Tax Reform, Final Report to the President, J. Robert Kerrey chairman, John C. Danforth vice-chairman (Washington, D.C.: U.S. Government Printing Office, January 1995).

The commission sounds the alarm about our future. The principal chart included in the commission's final report—and adapted here as "Government Spending Out of Control"—best defines our problems. By the year 2030, just thirty-five years from now, Social Security and Medicare alone will consume all existing federal revenues, and more. As mentioned earlier, existing federal revenues total 19 percent of GDP. In those circumstances, to meet current commitments and pay interest on the debt, we will need to raise federal taxes to at least 38 percent of GDP by 2030. This is double the amount of present federal taxes.

Government spending *is* out of control, and our future is at risk.

No Security for Old or Young

Another way to define the scope of the problem is to look at the impact these trends will have on different generations. The way we're going, the interests of young workers and those of the baby boomers are in conflict.

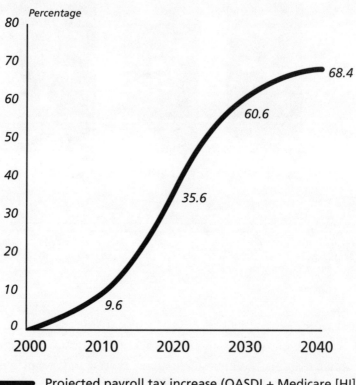

**Payroll Tax Increase on Youth
(to pay Present Law benefits to seniors)**

Percentage

Projected payroll tax increase (OASDI + Medicare [HI])

Source: Federal Old-Age and Survivors Insurance and Disability Insurance Trust Funds (OASDI), Board of Trustees, 1994 Annual Report, House Document 103-231 (Washington, D.C.: U.S. Government Printing Office, April 12, 1994).

The baby boomers have paid their money into Social Security and Medicare. They rightfully expect to receive their benefits. To pay these promised benefits, however, young workers will face a 68 percent payroll tax increase in 2040 and higher income taxes—and this, remember, is before paying state and local taxes. These increases mean, as shown earlier, that young workers can expect to pay a 60 percent lifetime tax rate. (See the figure "Payroll Tax Increase on Youth.") That's unacceptable.

Now look at the other side of the equation. Let's assume that we're *not* going to raise taxes on the young generation. What happens to the benefits for our senior citizens? (See the figure "Reduced Benefits for Seniors.")

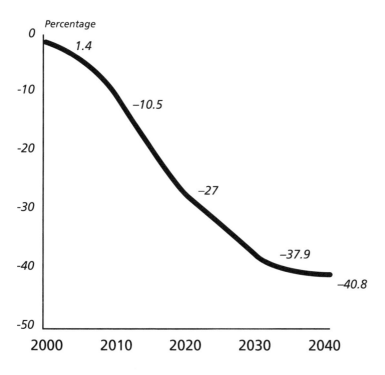

Reduced Benefits for Seniors

Percentage entitlement (OASDI + Medicare [HI]) benefit reduction assuming no payroll tax increase

Source: Federal Old-Age and Survivors Insurance and Disability Insurance Trust Fund (OASDI), Board of Trustees, 1994 Annual Report, House Document 103-231 (Washington, D.C.: U.S. Government Printing Office, April 12, 1994).

As you discovered in Chapter 3, if we don't raise taxes, baby boomers will suffer 40 percent cuts in Social Security and Medicare benefits. And *that's* unacceptable.

Under the old way of thinking, everyone stands to lose. A fair middle ground might seem to be to cut Social Security and Medicare 15 to 20 percent, and place a lifetime 40 percent tax-rate burden on the young. But all tax increases reduce savings and investment and impair economic growth. With reduced employment opportunities, we are all losers. I don't think this is anyone's vision of America—or the future any American wants.

WHAT CAN WE DO?

Simply stated, the times demand that we find whole new approaches. We need to go back to basics and rely on traditional American strengths— American ingenuity and private sector growth. Let's put the power of compound interest and private sector investment to work. Let's open the doors of capital ownership to all Americans. By cutting everyone in on the action, we can create positive alternatives and reignite hopes for a bright future.

In 2030, under the proposed new Tier 2 funded Social Security system, individuals who have worked a full thirty-five years, and have paid at least $1,560 per year into Social Security are projected to have $516,670 each in their personal investment and retirement accounts under Social Security. Individuals who work forty-five years (age twenty through age sixty-five) are projected to have $1,291,433. Individuals who work fifty years (age twenty through age seventy) are projected to have $2,005,799.

The assets of the individual investment and retirement accounts will be invested in the private economy. Many billions of dollars in new savings will make America grow and prosper, creating whole new industries and millions of new jobs. After the transition years, payroll taxes for Social Security can be cut two percentage points, then cut again— and we will be well on our way to creating 100 million millionaires.

The Promise of Capital Ownership

The best example of democratic capital ownership is home ownership. Sixty-one million Americans own their homes, with an average value of $80,000. Home ownership is a very important part of the American dream. Less widespread but equally exciting is small and independent business ownership. There are more than 21 million sole proprietorships, partnerships, and small businesses in America. American home and small business ownership is the envy of the world.

In contrast, capital ownership remains concentrated in a few hands. Under a revised pension system and a funded Social Security system, however, this pattern can change, and we can create 100 million millionaires. Capital ownership through Social Security and your pension can be ten times greater in value than home ownership—if from age twenty to age sixty-five or seventy you can set aside $25 to $30 a week to become a millionaire.

Two Ways to Become a Millionaire

This book offers the possibility of two alternative (and often complementary) ways to become a millionaire: through the existing pension system in the private or public sector and through the funded Tier 2 of the two-tier Social Security system—which will provide that you pay money each year into a personal investment and retirement fund in your name. In each case, if you set aside $25 to $30 per week during your working lifetime, you will be a millionaire when you retire.

Set aside $25 to $30 per week through your pension and $25 to $30 per week through a funded Social Security system, and you can be a millionaire twice over.

THE PRIVATE PENSION ALTERNATIVE

A pension offers you an immediate opportunity to save and build an important capital nest egg. You can start tomorrow. All the necessary laws and federal tax incentives to make you wealthy already exist. The money can be set aside pre-tax and can grow tax-free.

There are two drawbacks to the pension system, however. First, many employers, especially small businesses, can't (or won't) afford it. The concept is for you to set aside $10 a week—or $520 per year—and for your employer to set aside $20 a week—or $1,040 per year. Many employers will not set aside $1,040 for their employees.

Second, many families can't afford the $25 to $30 per week if their employers don't participate. Most families with incomes under $30,000, $40,000, or $50,000 have too many other financial pressures: the savings for retirement are not available. And America is a nation of consumers, not savers. Even families who *can* often *don't* set the money aside.

WHAT A FUNDED SOCIAL SECURITY SYSTEM WOULD MEAN TO YOU

Let's explore what a funded Social Security system would mean to you— in contrast to the existing pay-as-you-go-system. Current Social Security is a transfer payment. That is, none of the money you pay in is set aside for you. All of your money pays the benefits of current beneficiaries— yesterday's workers. When you retire, tomorrow's workers are expected to pay your benefits.

Likely Benefits under the Pay-as-You-Go System

Under the existing pay-as-you-go system, likely benefit levels by 2040 are uncertain. But there is one certainty. According to almost every scenario, there will have to be substantial cuts. Promised Present Law benefit levels cannot be sustained.

Nearly all experts dealing with this issue, however—ranging from the Advisory Council on Social Security to AARP—the American Association of Retired Persons—talk about finding a middle ground: raise payroll taxes two to four percentage points and cut benefits 10 to 15 percent. This can be called the "Half Tax/Half Cut" level of benefits. After the turn of the century, certainly by 2040, the

Half Tax/Half Cut level is the probable benefit level under the pay-as-you-go system. This level of benefits is the proper standard of comparison for a funded system.

Likely Benefits under a Funded System during the Transition

A major goal of this book is to stimulate a national debate on new approaches to update and remodel Social Security for the twenty-first century. The transition is sure to be a major theme of the debate. Under a funded system, the transition years require a delicate balancing act. We need to meet our promises to existing retirees, aged sixty-two to sixty-five and over, under Tier 1 traditional taxes.

During the transition years even younger workers will be allowed to set aside only a portion of their Social Security payments into their funded Tier 2 accounts. Part of everyone's payments will still be required to fund our commitments to existing retirees. The set-asides which I propose range from $500 up to $3,000 per year during the transition and include voluntary personal savings matches.

For individuals who are not yet retired, aged let's say forty to sixty-four today, the transition is very important. These individuals will not have enough time to build up sufficient capital in their retirement and savings accounts to pay likely Social Security benefits. In the beginning, most of their Social Security benefits will be paid through Tier 1 traditional payroll taxes. As the years go by, capital will slowly accumulate in the individual funded accounts under Tier 2. Increasingly, their Social Security benefits will be paid through income received from accumulated capital. Even in the transition years, a large majority of retirees will receive increased Social Security benefits if they purchase an annuity with their accumulated capital. Individuals under thirty-nine years of age today and future generations will realize the greatest benefits under a funded system.

Maximum Benefits under a Mature Funded System: A Sharp Contrast

To create a sharp contrast, let's compare Social Security benefits under the pay-as-you-go system to maximum benefits under a mature funded (after the transition) system. Let's assume that workers invest the same 12.4 percent of payroll into their funded accounts.

COMPARATIVE BENEFIT LEVELS

	Pay-as-You-Go		Mature Funded System	
Salary	Present Law	Expected benefits Half Tax/ Half Cut	With annuity	5% income
$20,000	$13,633	$11,967	$28,877	$18,277
$40,000	$21,209	$18,617	$57,755	$36,554
$60,000	$25,441	$22,309	$86,632	$54,831

- A $20,000 worker pays $2,480 per year to Social Security. After forty-five years, the worker is projected to have $2,053,048 in accumulated capital—$365,538 in today's value. The worker's benefits with an annuity will be $28,877 per year. At 5 percent income from capital, benefits will be $18,277 per year. Pay-as-you-go Present Law benefits are $13,633. Expected benefits at Half Tax/Half Cut levels are $11,967.

- A $40,000 worker pays $4,960 per year to Social Security. After forty-five years, the worker is projected to have $4,106,096 in accumulated capital—$731,076 in today's value. The worker's benefits with an annuity will be $57,755 per year. At 5 percent income from capital, benefits will be $36,554 per year. Pay-as-you-go Present Law benefits are $21,209. Expected benefits at Half Tax/Half Cut levels are $18,617.

- A $60,000 worker pays $7,440 per year to Social Security. After forty-five years, the worker is projected to have $6,159,144 in accumulated capital—$1,096,614 in today's value. The worker's benefits with an annuity will be $86,632 per year. At 5 percent income from capital, benefits will be $54,831 per year. Pay-as-you-go Present Law benefits are $25,441. Expected benefits at Half Tax/Half Cut levels are $22,309.

In developing this plan, I have used the 1994 *Annual Statistical Supplement to the Social Security Bulletin* (hereafter, the *Statistical Supplement*) to analyze the impact of a funded system on the 125 million wage and salary earners in the United States.

The plan I propose assumes that minimum participation in a funded system requires earning enough to pay $500 per year into Social Security—earned income of $4,032. Twenty-five million workers do not earn that much and are excluded from the analysis. (In a fully operational system, all workers, regardless of income level, will participate. But this cut-off level is appropriate for the present analysis. There are almost no workers who learn less than $4,032 a year *throughout their working lifetimes*.) This leaves 100 million participating workers as a base for the funded system.

What are the results?

- In a funded system, any individual who works forty-five years and earns **$10,000** or more per year will become a millionaire by age sixty-five.
- By the year 2000, more than 100 million Americans will be earning at least **$10,000** annually. They will pay **$1,240** per year each into Social Security and can become millionaires.
- In 2040, total capital assets of retirees will exceed **$6.8 trillion**.

Seventy million of the 100 million workers are expected to add a voluntary personal savings match. When they retire, if they purchase an annuity, their benefits will exceed Present Law levels by more than 60 percent. Their benefits will be nearly double the Half Tax/Half Cut benefit levels.

I believe that most workers will choose to retain their capital. They will own the capital and can pass it on tax-free to their heirs. During their retirement years, they should be able to receive 5 percent annual income from the capital. At the 5 percent income level, for the 70 million workers participating in the savings match, 85 percent of these will have benefit levels surpassing Half Tax/Half Cut. Sixty percent will surpass Present Law benefits, and this group will still have the $6.8 trillion to pass on to their heirs.

Thirty million of the 100 million workers may elect not to add a personal savings match. In this case, $500 per year of the taxes they are already paying will be set aside into their personal accounts. On retirement, if they purchase an annuity, 93 percent will have benefits exceeding Half Tax/Half Cut levels. One-third will surpass Present Law benefits.

UNDER A FUNDED SOCIAL SECURITY SYSTEM

Any individual
- who earns $10,000 or more
- and works forty-five years
- becomes a millionaire by age sixty-five

Please see the Appendix for a more detailed analysis. Please also review the following profiles to get a better sense of how the system will work. The men and women profiled are all real people whom I interviewed for this book.

Particularly illustrative is the profile of Brett Tracy, a short-order cook at a fast food restaurant. At a salary of $10,000, Brett, age twenty, would retire after forty-five years at age sixty-five under the reformed Social Security System with $1,026,524. After fifty years, Brett would retire with $1,594,353.

★   ★   ★

Profiles: Real People, Real Jobs

Brett Tracy

Salary $10,000 per year

Profession:	Short order cook
Type of Business:	Fast food restaurant
Age:	Twenty
Family Status:	Single
Education:	Will graduate from high school by year end 1996

A Comparison: Pay-as-You-Go Social Security vs. Funded Social Security

Current age	20
Years of set-asides	45
Today's salary	$10,000
Amount of set-aside per year	1,240
Capital accumulation at sixty-five	1,026,524
Today's value	182,769
Salary at retirement	15,236
Capital accumulation at seventy	1,594,353
Present Law benefits from Social Security	9,121
Safety Net benefits	6,892
Half Tax/Half Cut benefits	8,006
Funded Social Security:	
With annuity	14,439
At 5 percent income from capital	9,138
Plus income from Social Security payroll taxes*	0
	$9,138

PLUS CAPITAL ACCUMULATION $182,769

---

*If 5 percent income from capital is less than Safety Net benefits, Social Security will add the difference, so that benefits never drop below the Safety Net levels.

Brett speaks out

Are you on a treadmill?

Pretty much. But I'm pretty positive. I have my whole life in front of me.

On becoming a millionaire:

I never thought about it before. But I think so. If I had money, I don't think I would buy a lot of things. I would invest in a small business.

Are you optimistic or pessimistic about the future?

I'm optimistic. I tried to open my own nightclub. I had a business plan and everything. It didn't work out. But I'll do it some day.

On the soundness of Social Security:

I seriously doubt that it will be there for me. The government is so far in debt. The way they spend money, I don't see how.

If the government raises taxes to pay for Social Security?

I'm paying enough. I can't afford more taxes. As it is, they take a big chunk of my salary before I see anything. My car payments are $100 a month. I pay $160 a month for insurance. I can't afford it, and I don't have a family yet.

Will you have a greater opportunity than your parents?

Yes. My Mom never went to college. I'm hoping to finish high school next year, and go on to college some day.

And the opportunity for your children?

No. It's harder and harder to get a job and make a decent wage. Competition is tough. Everything is computerized and most people have less chance.

Current savings:

None. I had some savings, but spent them all on my car.

Do you have a pension?

No.

Hobbies and recreation:

I like ice skating. When I'm older, I'd like to get a pilot's license and learn to fly.

Karen Cherubini

Salary $15,000 per year

Profession:	Beauty technician
Type of Business:	Hair and nail salon
Age:	Twenty-six
Family Status:	Single parent—one son
Education:	High school graduate

A Comparison: Pay-as-You-Go Social Security vs. Funded Social Security

Current age	26
Years of set-asides	39
Today's salary	$15,000
Amount of set-aside per year	1,560
Capital accumulation at sixty-five	750,479
Today's value	169,072
Salary at retirement	21,578
Capital accumulation at seventy	1,181,157
Present Law benefits from Social Security	10,742
Safety Net benefits	8,084
Half Tax/Half Cut benefits	9,413
Funded Social Security:	
With annuity	13,357
At 5 percent income from capital	8,454
Plus income from Social Security	
payroll taxes	0
	$8,454

PLUS CAPITAL ACCUMULATION   *$169,072*

Karen speaks out

Are you on a treadmill?

It seems so. I work and work more hours. I don't seem to make any more. Especially as a single parent. I don't make enough. It's difficult.

On becoming a millionaire:

I don't believe you. But I'd love it. First I'd go on a shopping spree. Send my son to the best schools. Maybe buy a house in the Caribbean and travel.

Are you optimistic or pessimistic about the future?

I'm optimistic about my future. I see myself back in school. I look forward to getting married again. I am worried about my son's education and his safety on the streets.

On the soundness of Social Security:

That's a good question. From what people are saying, it won't be there for me. From the way the government is spending money, I doubt it'll be there.

If the government raises taxes to pay for Social Security?

The current taxes seem outrageous. The more I work, the more the government takes. What am I working for if I don't get any of it?

Will you have a greater opportunity than your parents?

No. People and times are different. You can't afford to buy a house. The world is too fast-paced.

And the opportunity for your children?

They'll have it harder. I will do everything I can to give my son a good education and values. I had every opportunity. But only the wealthy can afford to go to college, and that's where the opportunity is.

Current savings:

Less than $500. I'm trying. That was my New Year's resolution—to save more.

Do you have a pension?   No.

Hobbies and recreation: I enjoy arts and crafts and making wreaths out of silk flowers. Skiing. We go to the beach and surf cast for sand sharks, or go charter fishing for flounder and blue fish.

Ricardo Henry

Salary $40,000 per year

Profession:	Store manager
Type of Business:	Twenty-four hour convenience store
Age:	Thirty
Family Status:	Single parent—one son
Education:	High school graduate—three years of college

A Comparison: Pay-as-You-Go Social Security vs. Funded Social Security

Current age	30
Years of set-asides	35
Today's salary	$40,000
Amount of set-aside per year	3,000
Capital accumulation at sixty-five	993,595
Today's value	261,864
Salary at retirement	55,381
Capital accumulation at seventy	1,581,931
Present Law benefits from Social Security	19,273
Safety Net benefits	14,663
Half Tax/Half Cut benefits	16,968
Funded Social Security:	
With annuity	22,257
At 5 percent income from capital	13,093
Plus income from Social Security	
payroll taxes	1,570
	$14,663

PLUS CAPITAL ACCUMULATION $ 261,864

Ricardo speaks out

Are you on a treadmill? Yes and no. I stay really busy, and I think I'm getting ahead. At the same time, I'm not a college graduate. A college degree today is what a high school diploma used to be. Unless you know somebody, or get lucky, it's hard to get ahead.

On becoming a millionaire: Yeah. I think I could. It all depends on saving and wise investments. I would buy a new home. I would give money to others. I don't think I would change my life much.

Are you optimistic or pessimistic about the future? The way I see things going, they don't look too promising.

On the soundness of Social Security: When I retire, I don't think it will be there. The way the deficit is going, we're getting deeper and deeper in debt. It especially won't be there for my son's son.

If the government raises taxes to pay for Social Security? We have to do what we have to do. The average American is earning $20,000 to $25,000, and raising taxes is tough; but there may be a need. There's a lot of waste. We need tighter security on food stamps and people on welfare who don't try to get a job.

Will you have a greater opportunity than your parents? No. My father was a supervisor at a big company. My mother was a research assistant. They're both retired. They did well. I'm making less.

And the opportunity for your children? Our kids take too much for granted. With the military, I've been to Japan and around the world. Those kids are hungry. They go to school year-round. Unless we make changes, we're going to be caught behind.

Current savings: $14,000 including profit sharing.

Do you have a pension?   Yes. A 401(k). I don't know how much
                                money is in it. I get a statement every
                                June. I look at it every now and then, but
                                I don't know the amount.

Hobbies and Recreation: My son is four. I love playing with him—
                                taking him to the park. We watch *The
                                Lion King* tape together. I like exercising. I
                                run two miles a day and lift weights. My
                                best is bench pressing 335 pounds with
                                two repetitions.

★   ★   ★

Shelly and Renée Hargrove

Salaries $17,300 and $19,500 per year

Shelly approved being included in the book but did not want his picture to appear: "I don't want people seeing me all over the country."

Profession:	Both are house maintenance professionals.
Type of Business:	Both are health care workers, at different hospitals.
Ages:	Thirty and thirty-three
Family Status:	Married—three children, ages: two, six, and thirteen
Education:	High school graduates

A Comparison: Pay-as-You-Go Social Security vs. Funded Social Security

	Shelly	Renée
Current age	33	30
Years of set-asides	32	35
Today's salary	$17,300	$19,500
Amount of set-aside per year	1,560	1,560
Capital accumulation at sixty-five	387,494	516,670
Today's value	114,876	136,169
Salary at retirement	23,275	26,998
Capital accumulation at seventy	684,275	833,604
Present Law benefits from Social Security	10,962	12,184
Safety Net benefits	8,571	9,269
Half Tax/Half Cut benefits	9,766	10,726
Funded Social Security: With annuity	11,902 +	13,218
At 5 percent income from capital	5,744 +	6,808
Plus income from Social Security payroll taxes	2,827 +	2,461
	$8,571 +	$9,269

PLUS CAPITAL ACCUMULATION $114,876 + $136,169

Shelly speaks out

Are you on a treadmill?	Paying our bills is tough. Rent. Gas. Electric. The car note. Food. The kids and their clothes. When you get done, there's nothing left.
On becoming a millionaire:	I couldn't be a millionaire. I'd like it [big smile]. I'd like to become rich. Do all the things I can't do now. Go on a boat ride. Travel. Help other people. If I was a millionaire, I'd really be free [big laugh].
Are you optimistic or pessimistic about the future?	The way I see things going, they don't look too promising.
On the soundness of Social Security:	No. By the time I get old, the money won't be there.
If the government raises taxes to pay for Social Security?	Every time they talk about raising taxes, I get angry. They're taking too much now. That's just more money out of my check and I never see it.
Will you have a greater opportunity than your parents?	Yes. I have more money than my parents. My father taught art at school. My mother was a housewife.
And the opportunity for your children?	We're doing everything so that our kids will be better off. I see them graduating from college and going on to be doctors, nurses, teachers, or lawyers.
Current savings:	None.
Do you have a pension?	No.
Hobbies and recreation:	I love spooky movies and all sorts of sports. I love playing football and basketball with the kids.

Donna Hurst

Salary $16,000 per year

Profession:	Accounting clerk
Type of Business:	Car dealership
Age:	Thirty-one
Family Status:	Married—no children
Education:	High school graduate—two years of college

A Comparison: Pay-as-You-Go Social Security vs. Funded Social Security

Current age	31
Years of set-asides	34
Today's salary	$16,000
Amount of set-aside per year	1,560
Capital accumulation at sixty-five	469,804
Today's value	128,771
Salary at retirement	21,942
Capital accumulation at seventy	750,479
Present Law benefits from Social Security	10,646
Safety Net benefits	8,174
Half Tax/Half Cut benefits	9,410
Funded Social Security:	
With annuity	11,908
At 5 percent income from capital	6,439
Plus income from Social Security payroll taxes	1,735
	$8,174

PLUS CAPITAL ACCUMULATION $128,771

Donna speaks out

Are you on a treadmill?

If you're born middle class, you stay middle class. It's hard to break out unless you hit the lottery or invent something important. The chances are—you're stuck. My parents were middle class. I grew up middle class, and that's where I'll remain.

On becoming a millionaire:

Sure. I believe it. Right now my taxes are going into a system that's losing money. If my Social Security taxes were invested properly, I could be a millionaire. What would I do? I'd pay off my debts. Go see the world. I love horses. I would help handicapped people ride.

Are you optimistic or pessimistic about the future?

I'm worried about all the money the government is spending.

On the soundness of Social Security:

That's questionable. In another forty years, it might still be there. The way our government is spending money, we could be so far in debt that we'll be a third-rate nation.

If the government raises taxes to pay for Social Security?

I can't afford to pay more taxes, but what choice do I really have? If they're going to raise taxes, they should reduce the national debt. If they raise taxes—if the public thought it would really do something—I could probably buckle down a little more. Not that I want to.

Will you have a greater opportunity than your parents?

In some ways yes. Both men and women growing up have more possibilities than our parents. But inflation is eating us up.

And the opportunity for your children?

The government is spending our future. If we ran our family the way they run the government, they'd take us to debtor's prison. Unless we change, our children will be worse off. Good job opportunities are disappearing. And I can't afford to send my kids to a good college, which is essential for them to have a chance.

Current savings: Less than $1,000 in a bank, and I have about $1,000 in stocks.

Do you have a pension? No.

Hobbies and recreation: We live in the country on eleven acres. My horse is my recreation. My husband and I love motorcycle riding.

Richard Fayson

Salary $14,000 per year

Profession:	Machine operator and blender
Type of Business:	Chemical compounding
Age:	Twenty
Family Status:	Single
Education:	High school graduate

A Comparison: Pay-as-You-Go Social Security vs. Funded Social Security

Current age	20
Years of set-asides	45
Today's salary	$14,000
Amount of set-aside per year	1,560
Capital accumulation at sixty-five	1,291,433
Today's value	229,935
Salary at retirement	21,330
Capital accumulation at seventy	2,005,799
Present Law benefits from Social Security	10,926
Safety Net benefits	8,255
Half Tax/Half Cut benefits	9,590
Funded Social Security:	
With annuity	18,165
At 5 percent income from capital	11,497
Plus income from Social Security payroll taxes	0
	$11,497

PLUS CAPITAL ACCUMULATION   *$229,935*

Richard speaks out

Are you on a treadmill?	I really can't say. When you're young everything seems okay. And I don't have a family yet. Even now, it's hard to live. You have to struggle to pay bills.
On becoming a millionaire:	I believe so. If I were rich, I'd get seventy dogs. I love dogs. And spend money on my family.
Are you optimistic or pessimistic about the future?	It seems like America is going downhill fast, and no one is trying to stop it. When you leave your house, you have to worry about getting to your car. You don't even know if your car will be there.
On the soundness of Social Security:	I don't know. They're talking about cutting Social Security. It's not fair to cut people off after they've paid in and worked all their lives.
If the government raises taxes to pay for Social Security?	Taxes are already high enough. I got enough trouble paying my bills without giving more to the government.
Will you have a greater opportunity than your parents?	Probably not. Things are different. My parents didn't start with much, and they worked hard for everything they got. My dad's an auditor, and my mom is a machine operator. When we grew up, we had things pretty easy. We don't know how to work as hard.
And the opportunity for your children?	I think my children will have less opportunity. Every parent wants their kids to be everything they can be. But if there are no good jobs out there, what will they do?
Current savings:	None.
Do you have a pension?	No.
Hobbies and recreation:	Lifting weights. Playing basketball. My dog. Partying.

Larry and Michelle Hahn

Salaries $55,000 and $27,500 per year

Professions:	Commercial insurance salesman; assistant office manager/accountant/bookkeeper
Type of Business:	Insurance; industrial heating, air conditioning company
Ages:	Thirty-one and twenty-eight
Family Status:	Married—no children yet
Education:	College graduate; high school graduate—two-year business school, associate degree

A Comparison: Pay-as-You-Go Social Security vs. Funded Social Security

	Larry	Michelle
Current age	31	28
Years of set-asides	34	37
Today's salary	$55,000	$27,500
Amount of set-aside per year	3,000	2,500
Capital accumulation at sixty-five	903,469	999,233
Today's value	247,636	243,482
Salary at retirement	75,424	38,810
Capital accumulation at seventy	1,443,229	1,581,243
Present Law benefits from Social Security	21,945	15,762
Safety Net benefits	16,848	11,927
Half Tax/Half Cut benefits	19,396	13,844
Funded Social Security: With annuity	24,029 +	19,235
At 5 percent income from capital	12,382 +	12,174
Plus income from Social Security payroll taxes	4,467 +	0
	$16,848 +	$12,174

PLUS CAPITAL ACCUMULATION $247,636 + $243,482

Larry speaks out

Are you on a treadmill?	We're getting ahead, but not as fast as we'd like. As we make more money, we seem to have more bills. We're buying an investment property, and this will add to our income.
On becoming a millionaire:	I'm familiar with compound interest. I'm confident we can. This will help us in our retirement. We can travel. Mostly this will give us a legacy to pass on to our kids. Help them through college and buy a home.
Are you optimistic or pessimistic about the future?	Personally we're optimistic. Our salaries are increasing year by year. As well as our skills, confidence, and opportunities. We're not as optimistic about the country. Taxes are too high. Instead of pulling together everyone is out for themselves.
On the soundness of Social Security:	Our only input is our financial adviser. He says there's a good chance that Social Security won't be there for us.
If the government raises taxes to pay for Social Security?	Flat out—across the board—I'm against raising taxes for any reason. I'm not knowledgeable about where all our taxes are going, but Michelle and I only take home 65 percent to 68 percent of our money. One-third is enough for the government.
Will you have a greater opportunity than your parents?	Yes. Definitely. My father was a general foreman in a union electrician hall. My mother is a social worker. Our parents educated us well, and we're very grateful.
And the opportunity for your children?	I'm sketchy on that. A possibility. I have my doubts. The way our society is deteriorating, I tend to doubt it.

Current savings: Michelle and I are each putting $2,000
                                       per year into an IRA. That's our way of
                                       protecting our future.

Do you have a pension?   No. Our IRA is our pension.

Hobbies and recreation: We're both golfers and Notre Dame
                                       enthusiasts. We play racquetball, travel,
                                       and try to get away four times a year.

★   ★   ★

Melitza Rodriguez

Salary $13,000 per year

Profession:	Store manager
Type of Business:	Retail clothing store
Age:	Twenty-four
Family Status:	Single parent—two children, son, age five, daughter, age three
Education:	High school graduate

A Comparison: Pay-as-You-Go Social Security vs. Funded Social Security

Current age	24
Years of set-asides	41
Today's salary	$13,000
Amount of set-aside per year	1,560
Capital accumulation at sixty-five	901,159
Today's value	187,702
Salary at retirement	19,246
Capital accumulation at seventy	1,411,403
Present Law benefits from Social Security	10,465
Safety Net benefits	7,923
Half Tax/Half Cut benefits	9,194
Funded Social Security:	
With annuity	14,828
At 5 percent income from capital	9,385
Plus income from Social Security payroll taxes	0
	$9,385

PLUS CAPITAL ACCUMULATION $187,702

Melitza speaks out

Are you on a treadmill?	I do everything for my kids. It's a struggle, but I'm making it.
On becoming a millionaire	I won't believe it until I see it. The only way to get money like that is luck.
Are you optimistic or pessimistic about the future?	I haven't thought about it much. Young people are really having problems. There aren't enough jobs. We don't have enough experience.
On the soundness of Social Security:	I hope so. I really don't know.
If the government raises taxes to pay for Social Security?	The government is already taking a lot of taxes. We're struggling now. They shouldn't take any more.
Will you have a greater opportunity than your parents?	No. My parents own their own business. In the future, I hope so.
And the opportunity for your children?	I hope my children have a good chance. But everything is so hard, and getting harder. Years back, if you quit school, there were jobs. Now everything is computers. You have to finish school. To get where you want, you even need a Master's.
Current savings:	I've spent most of my savings. I have less than $100 in my savings account. I need to build it back up.
Do you have a pension?	No.
Hobbies and recreation:	I like playing with the kids and taking them to the park. I like going out and partying.

You may want to compare these profiles with the Illustration of Levels table.

THE PROMISE OF CAPITAL OWNERSHIP • 67

LEVELS OF PARTICIPATION

The plan for funded Social Security proposes six different levels of monies to be set aside into individual savings and retirement accounts:

The mandatory level for all participants:	$ 500
A range based on taxes you are already paying and a voluntary savings match:	
For workers earning	
$4,032–$12,579 (based on existing Social Security taxes from $500 up to 12.4 percent of wage):	from $500 up to $1,559
Three options for workers earning **$12,580** and above:	$1,560, $2,500, $3,000

The *Statistical Supplement* lists multiple salary levels—from $1–$3,599 to $3,600–$23,199, up to $46,800–$53,400, and then $54,000 and over. My proposal uses these same salary ranges but divides "$54,000 and over" into two levels—$54,000–$59,999, and then $60,000 and over.

My proposal estimates selected annual dollar set-aside levels for the number of workers at each of the twelve salary levels. The participating group totals 100 million workers.

The Social Security Administration assisted in my calculation of the Social Security benefits levels. These are presented in 1996 constant dollars for workers expected to retire in 2040. The benefit levels are broken down into Safety Net, Half-Tax/Half Cut, and Present Law promises. Retiring workers under the funded Social Security system I propose will have two options. They can live in retirement on the income from their capital at an expected 5 percent rate of return, and pass the capital tax-free on to their children and other heirs, or buy an annuity and expend all their capital during their own lifetimes.

For sixty-five year-olds, life expectancy for males and females averages eighteen years. Individuals reaching age sixty-five can expect to live to eighty-three. With an annuity, you can expect to receive a 7.9 percent annual return on your capital—roughly a 2.9 percent per year increase over retaining the capital. My proposed plan is designed to encourage you to retain your capital and pass it on to your heirs. But you will retain the right to purchase an annuity.

Illustration of Levels

	Today's salary ($)	Current age	Annual set-aside ($)	Capital accum. at 65 ($)	Today's value ($)	Expected Benefits under regular SS; Half Tax/Half Cut ($)	Funded Social Security With annuity[a] ($)	5% Income[b] ($)
Worker 1	8,000	20	922	821,219	146,215	7,214	11,551	7,311
Worker 2	15,000	20	1,560	1,291,433	229,935	9,986	18,165	11,497
Worker 3	15,000	20	500[c]	413,921	73,697	9,986	10,733	8,596
Worker 4	20,000	30	1,560	516,670	136,169	10,907	13,374	9,425
Worker 5	30,000	20	2,500	2,069,605	368,486	15,927	29,110	18,424
Worker 6	50,000	40	2,500	306,338	119,509	17,955	20,115	16,649
Worker 7	60,000	20	3,000	2,483,526	442,183	22,309	34,932	22,109
Worker 8	60,000	40	3,000	367,606	143,411	19,583	22,318	18,159

a. If a worker chooses an annuity, he or she receives the Safety Net benefit levels plus 2.9% of capital exceeds this amount, the worker retains the surplus.

b. If 5% income from capital is less than the Safety Net benefits, Social Security adds the difference so that benefits never drop below the Safety Net levels.

c. The first $500 a worker pays into Social Security automatically goes into his or her personal investment and retirement account. To get additional tax monies set aside into their accounts, workers have a voluntary personal savings match requirement. This row demonstrates the outcome if a worker remains at the $500 set-aside level. In the proposed plan, the assumption is that 70% participate with savings matches and 30% choose not to.

The Funded Social Security System in Brief

A funded Social Security offers all working Americans the best opportunity to accumulate wealth—especially families with incomes under $50,000.

You already know that when funded Social Security is in place, you will be able to set aside $500—and up to $3,000 per year in a personal retirement and investment account. *Anyone setting aside $1,240 per year can become a millionaire in one working lifetime and be assured of a comfortable standard of living after retirement.*

- Over **70 million** Americans currently pay **$1,560** and more into Social Security each year.
- Over **85 million** Americans currently pay more than **$1,000** into Social Security each year.
- By the year 2000, over **100 million** Americans will be earning **$10,000** or more. They will pay **$1,240** per year into Social Security—and can become the 100 million millionaires this book celebrates.

All individuals aged sixty-four and under, and not already retired, will be able to participate. As I proposed in Chapter 2, Social Security will become a two-tier system, in which Tier 1 will continue to be pay-as-you-go. Most of your Social Security taxes will be pledged to pay the

Your Property Rights

A measure of the distrust created toward government is that people who have previewed this book raise the ownership issue again and again. They are skeptical. Somehow government, they believe, will try to get their hands on the capital in your individual portfolios.

◆

The U.S. Supreme Court in Fleming v. Nestor (1960) has ruled that workers (under current Social Security, without private accounts) have no legal claim to future Social Security benefits.

◆

A major difference in the proposed plan is that the money will be your property. No politician will have any legal claim to invade your account.

BELIEVE IT

The money set aside into a personal savings and retirement account under Social Security will be yours. You will have a property right in the account and legal title to the money.

◆

The government will not be able to borrow against your money or use it to pay its bills.

◆

Why?

◆

100 million voters would erupt in protest if the government invaded their private accounts.

Social Security of existing retirees, and this pledge will be kept. A portion of your Social Security taxes will go into the funded Tier 2.

Remember: Up to $3,000 per year will be paid into a funded personal investment and retirement account in your name. The money will be yours. This proposal enables you to become a millionaire, increases your retirement income, and provides a substantial inheritance to pass on to your heirs.

Financial Management

In the proposed system there is no pool of all monies. You will get annual statements showing your own current principal, your return on capital, and any administrative or management costs. There will be no surprises or hidden costs.

To allay any fears that the set-aside money can be tampered with, the president and Congress will establish an independent, private-public corporation—which I will discuss further in Chapter 7—to oversee the money and its management.

The responsibility of the financial managers will be modeled after the way asset managers serve existing large-scale government or corporate retirement pools today. The management goal will be to maintain a diversified investment portfolio seeking sustained long-term capital appreciation to benefit the participants for their retirement.

Benefits from Two Sources

Social Security benefits will be paid from two sources: Tier 1 (based on current payroll taxes) and Tier 2 (based on the interest income from accumulated capital) will combine to meet Social Security benefits. The structure of the two-tier system is explained in Chapter 7, "Save Social Security."

The pay-as-you-go Social Security system we now know will remain as a retirement safety net. When you retire, you will receive income from your accumulated capital at an estimated 5 percent rate of return. This interest income will be part of your promised Social Security benefit and will reduce that portion of your Social Security coming from current taxpayers.

For example, (in 1996 constant dollars), if you have $50,000 of capital in your Social Security investment and retirement account when you retire, you can expect to receive $2,500 (a 5 percent rate of return on capital per year for life, indexed to keep up with inflation). The average 1996 Social Security promised benefit is $10,088. The remaining $7,588 will come from the Tier 1, pay-as-you-go system from current, tax-paying employees. If your capital account is smaller, your interest income will be less; and more Tier 1, pay-as-you-go tax dollars will be required to meet your promised Social Security benefits. As the Tier 2 system matures and more capital is accumulated, the interest income

WHAT IF?

Think about the people you know. Think of yourself, your spouse. Think of your children. Think of your friends. Think of the people you work with.

What effect would this income have on the consumer economy? On starting a new business? On home ownership? On further education?

◆

◆

What if each of them had a $500,000 nest egg? Let's assume that the $500,000 adds $25,000 per year to their income. Each has an extra $2,083 per month to spend.

What would happen to the quality of your life and the life of your children and friends? What would happen to your sense of independence?

◆

from capital will increase and then surpass the Social Security benefit. You will retain all income which exceeds the Safety Net benefits.

As I have stated before, current retirees will be safeguarded and will continue to receive their promised benefits. The two-tier approach will protect all beneficiaries during the transition period. Someone aged forty-four, fifty-four, or sixty-four today, for example, will be secure during the transition under this phased system.

THE FINANCIAL MODEL

As noted earlier in the chapter, this book suggests two ways for you to become a millionaire—either under the proposed Tier 2 funded Social Security system or through a private or public pension. The basic concept is to set aside $25 to $30 per week during your working lifetime—and after forty-five to fifty years, you will be a millionaire.

The Option 3 table traces the growth of $30 per week at a 6 percent, 8 percent, and 10 percent compound interest rate. (These calculations include a 5 percent annual increase in the payments to keep up with inflation and real wage increases, as I explain below.) With a compound rate of return, your money is working for you all the time. Your money is making money. The result of this multiplication is six to twenty times higher than people often estimate.

The option tables are designed to give you an easy-to-follow picture of what funded Social Security will mean to you. These tables clearly demonstrate your possible economic future and are vitally important to you. These are the basic numbers underlying the whole thesis of this book.

Select the set-aside, rate of return, and number of years which best fit your circumstances. If you set aside $10, $20, or $30 per week, what happens? Suppose that you set the money aside for five, ten, fifteen, twenty, twenty-five, thirty, thirty-five, forty, forty-five, or fifty years. What happens to your money as time goes by? Assume different annual rates of growth—6 percent (conservative), 8 percent (intermediate), or 10 percent.

To make the numbers real, and relate them to your working lifetime, I have added inflation at an expected 4 percent per year and real wage growth at an expected 1 percent per year. What this means is that the

Option 1: Set Aside $10 per Week

Year	6% Return $Nominal	$Real	8% Return $Nominal	$Real	10% Return $Nominal	$Real
5	3,325	2,842	3,493	2,986	3,672	3,138
10	8,712	6,121	9,629	6,765	10,666	7,494
15	17,124	9,889	19,944	11,517	23,355	13,487
20	29,925	14,204	36,784	17,459	45,676	21,680
25	49,039	19,131	63,718	24,858	84,143	32,826
30	77,163	24,742	106,148	34,037	149,493	47,935
35	118,071	31,118	172,223	45,390	259,377	68,359
40	177,017	38,346	274,201	59,398	442,750	95,909
45	261,303	46,524	430,478	76,645	747,040	133,008
50	381,043	55,762	668,600	97,844	1,249,838	182,903

Option 2: Set Aside $20 per Week

Year	6% Return $Nominal	$Real	8% Return $Nominal	$Real	10% Return $Nominal	$Real
5	6,650	5,684	6,987	5,972	7,343	6,277
10	17,424	12,242	19,259	13,531	21,333	14,988
15	34,248	19,777	39,888	23,034	46,710	26,974
20	59,850	28,407	73,568	34,919	91,352	43,359
25	98,077	38,262	127,437	49,716	168,286	65,652
30	154,326	49,485	212,297	68,073	298,986	95,870
35	236,141	62,236	344,446	90,780	518,753	136,719
40	354,034	76,691	548,403	118,795	885,499	191,817
45	522,606	93,048	860,956	153,290	1,494,080	266,015
50	762,087	111,525	1,337,199	195,687	2,499,677	365,805

$10, $20, or $30 weekly set-aside needs to rise 5 percent per year to keep up with inflation and real wage growth. In this manner the set-aside remains the same percentage of your wage over time. The money you are setting aside each year retains the same value.

Option 3: Set Aside $30 per Week

| Year | 6% Return | | 8% Return | | 10% Return | |
	$Nominal	$Real	$Nominal	$Real	$Nominal	$Real
5	9,975	8,526	10,480	8,958	11,015	9,415
10	26,135	18,362	28,888	20,296	31,999	22,482
15	51,371	29,666	59,832	34,551	70,065	40,461
20	89,775	42,611	110,353	52,378	137,028	65,039
25	147,116	57,393	191,155	74,574	252,429	98,478
30	231,489	74,227	318,445	102,110	448,479	143,806
35	354,212	93,353	516,670	136,169	778,130	205,078
40	531,051	115,037	822,604	178,193	1,328,249	287,726
45	783,909	139,572	1,291,433	229,935	2,241,120	399,023
50	1,143,130	167,287	2,005,799	293,531	3,749,515	548,708

TURNING $25 TO $30 A WEEK INTO $1 MILLION

Let's use the financial model to see how you can turn $25 to $30 per week into more than $1 million. We can start with the specific amount of $30 per week.

That is, assume that between you and your employer, either through Tier 2 Social Security or the pension system, you can start to set aside $30 per week. Over the years, as inflation and real wages increase (recall that the model uses 4 percent for inflation and 1 percent for real wage increases each year) the $30 will have to increase to keep up with purchasing power, but as a percentage of wages, the set-aside remains exactly the same. Assume that under Social Security you pay half and your employer pays half and that in a pension plan assume you pay one-third and your employer pays two-thirds.

According to the model, each year the equivalent of $1,560 in 1996 current dollars is being invested for you. Assume you begin working at age twenty and end your career at age sixty-five to seventy—this is a period of forty-five to fifty years. After forty-five to fifty years, how much money will you have? Most people figure forty to fifty times $1,500—that's about $75,000—and add some interest, maybe double the money. The usual answer is in the range of $150,000. But here is the right answer:

- At an 8 percent compound rate of return, if you set aside $30 a week for **forty-five** years, you will have **$1,291,433**.
- At an 8 percent compound rate of return, if you set aside $30 a week for **fifty** years, you will have **$2,005,799**.

In reality, the average rate of return on the Standard and Poor's 500 has been 10.19 percent over the past seventy years—including the Great Depression.

The basis of the reformed Social Security and private pension systems this book proposes is to put the normal private sector investment rate of return to work for you.

YOUR FUTURE PURCHASING POWER

As you trace your potential capital growth in the option tables, you can always bring the amount of capital back to today's value (the $Real column subtracts 4 percent inflation) to gain a fair comparison: How much would your capital be worth today?

The dream of becoming a millionaire in America remains magical. The future value of your capital after forty-five and fifty years, whether it grows at 6 percent, 8 percent, or 10 percent is substantial. But expected inflation over the forty-five to fifty-year period will decrease the purchasing power of that money. To determine the purchasing power of those dollars today, you need to discount inflation—that is, allow for the likelihood that $1 million today buys more than $1 million will buy fifty years from now. Determining today's value gives you a good idea of your future purchasing power using future money.

As we have seen previously, yearly set-asides of at least $1,560 for fifty years are expected to grow to $2,005,799. This amount in the year 2046, adjusted for expected inflation, is the equivalent of $293,531 in 1996 dollars. With a $293,531 capital base today, taking 5 percent interest income only, you receive $14,677 per year for your lifetime and can pass the $293,531 on to your children—they'll be able to receive this inheritance tax-free if the reforms proposed in this book are adopted.

FUTURE OPTIONS

Once we get through the transition years, we, as Americans, will gain many positive options. Set-asides could increase substantially and even double for most workers. This will allow you to choose new alternatives.

Once the capital accumulation level in your individual funded account exceeds agreed-to retirement requirements, excess capital could be used to:

- help you upgrade your skills and train for new, higher-paying jobs
- help you pay for new educational opportunities for your children and grandchildren
- assist in creating savings for medical emergencies
- help you buy a home
- finance a business of your own
- provide emergency resources to pay living expenses during unexpected periods of unemployment or transition

The first priority for each of us will be to build sufficient income for retirement. The first purpose of the capital must be to provide for retirement needs, and regulations will provide that retirement funds cannot be used for any other purpose. But once sufficient capital has been accumulated for retirement, individuals could have control over their surplus for a series of approved options. The Singapore system, as described in Chapter 8, furnishes a good example of using excess capital for alternative economic opportunities.

AMERICA AT A CROSSROADS

The plan proposed in this book embodies a vision of economic opportunity and growth, a vision of an expanding America: Open the portals of capital ownership to all Americans, and we can enter a new period of economic prosperity.

The driving force behind America's wealth is investment in the private sector. We must bring federal spending into balance. Then a Tier 2 funded Social Security system and an expanded pension system will generate over $200 billion of *new* investment every year in the private sector. The economic pie will grow substantially, and the hopes and dreams of individual Americans will remain alive.

The alternative is to view the economy in narrow and fixed terms. Many Social Security proponents strongly argue that all Social Security needs is a few minor adjustments: Raise taxes two to four percentage points, cut benefits, and the pay-as-you-go system will remain in balance for seventy-five years. If recent history repeats, in ten to twenty years, all we will need to do is raise taxes again.

A Shrinking America

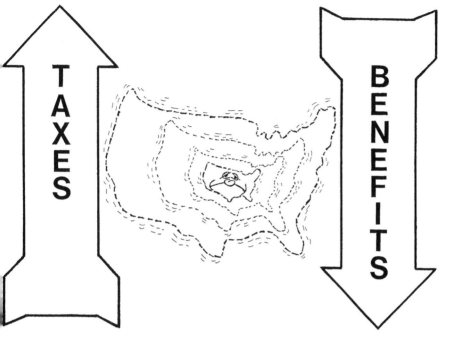

The Current Pay-as-You-Go System

Raise taxes. Cut benefits. Reduce savings. Slow economic growth. Lower our hopes for the future.

Advocates for leaving Social Security as it is don't want to discuss Medicare, because Medicare bills show major increases every year. These advocates see promised federal health benefits as a separate subject. But to pay for health promises, we will have to increase taxes an additional five percent, maybe even ten percent. To date we aren't at all close to capping spiraling medical costs.

Little by little, the lifeblood is being sucked out of our economy. Fewer and fewer resources are available to invest in new industries and new jobs. As we compete in the world, we need maximum resources to invest in new plant and equipment and in education. Yet these exact

A Growing America

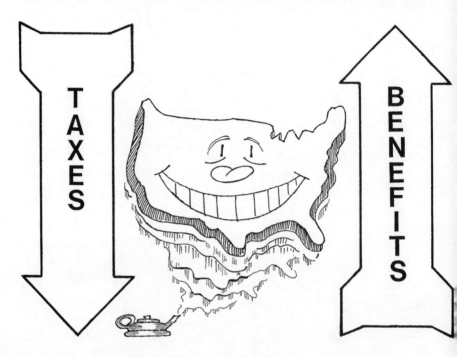

TAXES

BENEFITS

100 Million Funded Accounts under Social Security

Cut taxes. Raise benefits. Substantially increase savings. Expand the economy. Pass a brighter future on to our children.

monies are increasingly consumed by federal expenditures, and middle-class America is feeling the pinch.

Financing Social Security presents us with a stark choice—a shrinking America or a growing America. We have come to a crossroads, and we must choose which way to go. This book points in the direction of economic expansion and security, rather than a constantly narrowing opportunity and an intergenerational fight between young and old. If we open capital opportunity to all, the promise of America will remain firm.

PRINCIPLES OF FINANCIAL INDEPENDENCE

Find Out Where You Stand

What's the big deal about retirement income and life expectancy? Probably most people would rather think about something else—maybe sports or love. Every Sunday in the fall, more than a million people go to stadiums in the sun, rain, heat, or freezing cold to see the San Francisco Forty-niners, the New York Giants, and the Dallas Cowboys play football. Millions of Americans watch the daily soap operas on television, lured by the major themes of love and lust.

By comparison, calculating income after retirement is rarely a hot topic of conversation. Filling a room with a hundred people to discuss savings, pensions, and future Social Security benefits is difficult. But the importance of these matters becomes clear if you ask yourself a few simple questions: How much money do I need to live comfortably after I retire? How long can I expect to live?

People work all their lives and look forward to the "golden years." They see retirement as a time to really enjoy themselves. They think, "At last I'm free. I'll have the time to do everything I always wanted." But most things people enjoy cost money—eating in restaurants, going to the movies, shopping, travel, buying clothes, having friends over, pursuing hobbies.

Each person can calculate the probability of economic security or hardship after retirement. To find out where you stand, use the "Income after Retirement" worksheet. For the most part, how much money you think you will need to live comfortably after retirement will depend on the expectations you have built up as a result of your earning power during your working lifetime.

Income after Retirement:
Economic Security or Hardship?

Will you have economic security after retirement, or are you facing a serious income gap? Make your own calculations.

"To live comfortably after I retire, I project that I will need an annual income of . . . "

Check the appropriate level:

$ 5,000–$10,000	_____
$10,000–$20,000	_____
$20,000–$30,000	_____
$30,000–$50,000	_____
$50,000 and above	_____

Then calculate whether there is a gap.

Enter your earning power before retirement. $_____ per year

Enter the income you hope to have after retirement. $_____ per year

Subtract anticipated income from your pension (if available). $_____ per year

Subtract expected Social Security benefits per year. $_____ per year

(Average Social Security income for people retiring in 1996 is $10,088 per year, or $840.66 per month.)

Subtract expected annual contributions from accumulated savings, earnings, or other assets. $_____ per year

INCOME GAP $_____ per year

Tom Woodruff, the former executive director of President Jimmy Carter's Commission on Pension Policy, offers a simple and easy-to-follow rule of thumb. His belief is that most Americans wish to maintain the standard of living in retirement that they achieved in the final years of their employment. He estimates that to accomplish this Americans need to plan to have a retirement income equal to 75 percent to 85 percent of their highest pay—usually attained during their last working years.

Woodruff sees some costs going down during retirement—children are usually independent, the cost of home payments is lower, and there are no more FICA payments. At the same time, other costs—such as health care and leisure—will go up. And the biggest worry for those on fixed incomes is the loss of spending power due to erosion by inflation.

One standard to help you calculate and plan a "comfortable" income level for after retirement is to determine 75 percent to 85 percent of your highest income. Now compare the income level you selected to live comfortably after retirement with your projected income from Social Security. For those retiring in 1996, the average Social Security payment is $840.66 per month, or $10,088 per year. How does this compare with your recommended "comfortable" income level? Statistics collected from Social Security paint a stark picture of the so-called promise of our golden years:

- In 1992, **9.2 million** elderly Americans—22 percent of all seniors—had individual or family incomes under **$10,000**.
- In 1992, **14.8 million** elderly Americans—44.7 percent of all seniors—had individual or family incomes under **$15,000**.

Seniors with incomes under $15,000 are living on the edge. Their lifestyles include very little room for error or "comfort." They face constant financial worry. Fear of health problems creates a nonstop concern. Many older individuals own their homes. This lowers their expenses, because they have no mortgage or rent to pay; but owning a home includes surprise repairs and expensive upkeep—not covered in a $10,000 budget.

In focus groups I held while conducting research for this book, the participants reached the following simple conclusions about economic security: Social Security offers an invaluable baseline, but economic security requires each of us to have substantial additional retirement income. Some type of pension is an absolute necessity for a standard of living above the poverty level.

The statistics I've presented in this chapter provide all of us—individuals planning ahead for our senior years and national policy

LIFE EXPECTANCY

Please answer the following question:

After I retire, I expect to live ———— years.

The following statements summarize the aging revolution in terms of numbers, percentages, and life expectancy. They are important guides for you to help you figure how long you might live and what you can expect:

- Between 1900 and 1990 there was a major increase in life expectancy. The average life expectancy in 1900 was **47.3** years. The average life expectancy in 1989 was **75.2** years.
- The average life expectancy was **27.9** years higher in 1989 than in 1900. In 1930 one out of every twenty Americans was sixty-five and over. Forty years later, by 1970, one of every ten Americans was sixty-five and over. By the year 2030, one out of every five Americans is projected to be sixty-five and over.
- Most dramatically, in 2000, the average male and female

who reach age sixty-five can expect to live **17.4** more years—into their mid-eighties.
- Between 1990 and 2050 an additional **47.6 million** middle-aged Americans will be living. This represents an increase from **31.2 million** seniors in 1990 to **78.8 million** in 2050.
- In 100 years, from 1950 to 2050, the number of aged Americans will have increased two and one-half times as a percentage of the total population—from **8.2** percent in 1950 to **20.6** percent in 2050.

makers—with dramatic evidence underlining the imperative need for an adequate Social Security and pension system for all working Americans.

To continue to find out where you stand, figure out how long you expect to live after you retire. See the "Life Expectancy" box, which includes major longevity statistics. Many, many articles and books have been written on the need for economic security for seniors. They contain statistics from the Bureau of the Census about life expectancy and aging, but, understandably, the dry, statistical nature of these pages lulls the average reader into a comatose state, and the reader is not able to feel that the information is pertinent. But basic reality is simple: If you want to live the last twenty to thirty years of your life close to poverty or with constant financial worry, don't plan for your retirement. The issue of life expectancy is directly connected to the issue of income levels. The longer you live, the more important having a "comfortable" income level becomes. One option is to say, "I don't have enough income for retirement, but it doesn't matter too much, because I really don't expect to live too long after I retire." Facts point the other way.

Dan McGill in his book *The Fundamentals of Private Pensions,* which is considered the bible of pension literature, summarizes changes in Americans' life expectancy:

> During the last sixty years or so the growth in number and proportion of the aged population in the United States has been phenomenal. During that period the general population of the United States has doubled, while the number of persons aged sixty-five and over has quintupled. In 1920, there were roughly 4.9 million persons aged sixty-five and over, whereas sixty years later the number had grown to 25.9 million. . . . In relative terms, only 4.6 percent of the population in 1920 was sixty-five and over, whereas in 1980, 11.3 percent of the population fell in that category. It is estimated that from 17.5 to 25.6 percent of the population will be sixty-five and over by the year 2030.

It may be more fun to think about sports and love, but planning for retirement income and extended living is vital for your future well-being.

Save Social Security

By now you know it really is possible to become a millionaire in one working lifetime through Social Security, using your own money. Not only is it possible with some reforms of the system, but the changes will make Social Security stronger and healthier for the future. Of all the chapters in this book, this one is the most important to you. It is a must-read for everyone—but especially for any family with an income under $50,000.

The Vital Importance of Social Security

America has created a sacred contract through Social Security. Seniors have the right to know that Social Security will be solvent and available to assure their financial security after retirement. Nearly all pension experts endorse the importance of Social Security for the elderly. In *Pensions in a Changing Economy*, edited by Richard Burkhauser and Dallas Salisbury, Virginia Reno sums up: "Social Security has been and will continue to be the most important source of income in old age for the great majority of Americans." Research on income received by the elderly underlines how dependent elderly Americans are on Social Security. Ninety-two percent of elderly Americans receive Social Security.

Social Security is particularly vital for individuals in the lower two quintiles—the bottom 40 percent of income. Elderly Americans in the lowest two quintiles receive between 75.7 and 79.3 percent of their total income from Social Security. It is also true that Social Security payments favor individuals in the lower two quintiles. On a proportional basis they receive more money than they paid in, while people in the highest two quintiles receive proportionally less. This feature of the existing system is designed to reduce poverty among the elderly and has been working well. In 1966, 29 percent of America's elderly were officially listed as living in poverty. By 1991, this dropped to 12 percent, and in the early 1980s poverty among the elderly dipped below poverty levels for the rest of the population. This favorable development is mostly due to Social Security.

BUSINESS AS USUAL WON'T WORK

As I pointed out in Chapter 3 (see Secret No. 7), the solvency of the Social Security system in fifteen to twenty-five years—by 2010–2020—is in serious doubt. Public dialogue about Social Security, which has received much recent media attention, underlines a growing awareness that Social Security is in serious trouble.

Even though government bureaucrats may prefer that this information remain obscure, the federal government includes all the facts in its standard reports—the truth is in there if someone wants to dig it out. My major sources for information about Social Security are the 1994 Social Security Trustees' Report; the 1994 *Green Book: Overview of Entitlement Programs,* prepared by the House Committee on Ways and Means; and the 1994 *Statistical Supplement.*

There are two major causes for concern. First, the number of workers supporting each retiree—called the dependency ratio—is seriously eroding. Second, the number of beneficiaries—mostly because of aging of the baby boomers—is multiplying.

- In 1945 there were more than **20** workers to support every beneficiary, and life expectancy was short.
- In 1995 there were only **3.1** workers for every beneficiary.
- By 2033, the dependency ratio is projected to go below **2** workers to support every beneficiary.

At the same time the number of Social Security (OASDI) beneficiaries is growing at unprecedented levels. The 1994 Social Security Trustees' Report projects:

- **43.8 million** beneficiaries in 1995
- **75.8 million** beneficiaries in 2025
- **89.5 million** beneficiaries in 2055

DEMOGRAPHIC FACTORS IN SOCIAL SECURITY SOLVENCY

Demographic factors determine the number of people working to support the number of retirees receiving benefits.

Fertility Rate

- If women are producing more children, there will be more workers to pay benefits to retired employees.
- Fertility rates after World War II reached a high of **3.61** in 1960.
- By 1993 fertility rates were reduced to 2.05, and they are expected to drop under **2.0** by 2005 and stabilize at **1.90**.

Net Immigration

- Net immigration also has an impact on the number of workers being taxed to pay Social Security for retirees.
- The Social Security trustees anticipate that the net number of immigrants will be **850,000** per year by the year 2000.

Life Expectancy

In Chapter 6 we examined life expectancy and retirement income.

But life expectancy is also important in determining costs.

- The longer people live, the longer they expect to receive Social Security.
- In 1940 life expectancy at birth was **61.4** years for men and **65.7** years for women. At age sixty-five men could expect to live **11.9** more years and women **13.4** more years.
- Today the elderly expect to live into their eighties. At age sixty-five, men can expect to live **15.4** more years, and women **19.2** more years.

Dependency Ratio

Combining these demographic factors, we can calculate the all-important dependency ratio—the number of people working to support retirees.

- By 1995 there were only **3.1** workers for every beneficiary, and the retirees are expected to live longer.
- As early as 2033 this number could sink below two workers supporting every retiree.

In just sixty years the number of beneficiaries will more than double, and life expectancy continues to increase. (Please see the box for key demographic and economic indicators determining the solvency of Social Security.)

ECONOMIC FACTORS IN SOCIAL SECURITY SOLVENCY

Economic factors determine the overall health of the economy. If the economy is growing and real wages are increasing, there is more leeway to pay Social Security at an acceptable rate of taxation.

- Understanding that demographic and economic factors influence each other is not difficult. Predicting future numbers beyond a short period of years is the complicated part.
- Determining Social Security solvency requires a thirty- to seventy-year projection.

Real Wages

A very significant economic indicator is real wages, because real wages include estimated economic growth, the impact of international competition, inflation, and productivity.

- If real wages are growing, there is more money to afford Social Security payments. If real wages are

shrinking, higher taxes are required.
- In the 1960s, with continued prosperity, real wages grew an average of 2.2 percent annually throughout the decade.
- In the 1980s, real wages grew an average of .72 percent during the decade. In 1988 Social Security actuaries used an assumed 2.3 percent annual real wage growth rate, which helped create an overly positive analysis.
- In the 1994 Social Security Trustees' Report, new analyses lowered projected real wage growth to 1 percent per year for the intermediate projection.

Projected Payroll Tax

By using these demographic and economic factors, Social Security can project solvency for years ahead and determine projected payroll taxes to cover costs.

You may remember my Secret No. 7—here is a reminder of the facts revealed there. In constant 1994 dollars, the Social Security Trustees' Report projects the following cash flow shortfalls:

- In 2013 OASDI costs will exceed OASDI income for the first time, creating the first (**$7.3 billion**) deficit.
- By 2025 the annual Social Security deficit will reach **$146 billion**.
- By 2040, the projected deficit will exceed **$225 billion** per year.

Advocates of keeping the Social Security system exactly as it is favor some combination of cutting benefits and raising taxes. Discussion papers prepared for the official 1994–1995 Advisory Council on Social Security consider raising OASDI taxes either 2.3 percent or 4.9 percent in 1998 to balance Social Security. Social Security advocates understand very well that federal health insurance (Medicare) costs place an even more serious tax burden on the American worker than Social Security. As a matter of convenience, the Social Security experts sidestep the Medicare issue as not being in their area. But the worker can't sidestep the proposed taxes for Social Security and the proposed additional taxes to cover Medicare.

The Social Security Trustees' Report again is the best source for estimated tax increases. That is where I found Secret No. 2 (Chapter 3): the information that by 2030, payroll taxes will have to be increased to 25.69 percent to meet OASDI and HI cost rates. Then, on top of that, as I have mentioned before, we will pay 20 percent to 30 percent federal income taxes. And we cannot forget that on top of *that* we pay state and local taxes. This level of taxation is not possible: Americans will not accept paying taxes of 50 to 60 percent. We must stop!

The real crisis in Social Security and the combined entitlement programs offers us a chance to consider fresh approaches. Business as usual really won't work.

As we have seen in Chapter 4, the constant raising of taxes every few years pits one generation of Americans against another—the young against the old. In addition, increasing taxes again and again is short-sighted, because the tax increases become a continually growing burden on the private sector economy—the engine that finances the whole system and the underlying jobs which create all the revenue.

Just when we need new investment and increased savings to help America compete in the new global economy, an aging America—through no fault of its own—is placing an extra burden on the entire economy. We need a new approach which will expand, not shrink, the economy.

As I have stated earlier, the purpose of designing a new system and presenting it in this book is to stimulate a national debate. We need to focus on the tensions being created by our changing demographics. We need to seek bold new approaches so that we can protect our senior citizens and their expectations, as well as pass on a land of hope and promise to our children.

The national debate should be about how our institutions and our government affect our values. Our institutions should be designed to foster hope, hard work, family strength, and self-reliance. Our Social Security system is at the core of that debate. The pay-as-you-go system has served us well for over sixty years. But I maintain that as America changes going into the twenty-first century, we should remodel Social Security to meet twenty-first-century needs. That is why I propose a funded system. The debate needs to examine which system best serves

- our savings rates, economic growth, and future jobs
- our desire for individual independence and a sense of control in our lives and families
- the opportunity for all Americans to build capital and wealth in a free market economy
- the need to keep taxes at acceptable levels

In this chapter—and later, in Chapter 11, "A Step-by-Step Plan," as well as in the Appendix—I present the elements of a detailed system. The purpose of the detail is to show clearly that the transition to a funded system is affordable, and to offer individual readers a specific idea of how they will benefit. Willingness to go into detail also stands as an open invitation for new ideas and suggestions for improvement.

THE TWO-TIER APPROACH CAN SAVE SOCIAL SECURITY

Let's go back to the basic underlying strength of America—our economy and the private sector. Let's put the growth capacity of the private sector to work to save Social Security. In Chapter 5 we saw that creating a new kind of Social Security system can make capital ownership a possibility for all Americans and generate unprecedented new levels of savings and capital accumulation. The two-tier approach can meet three major objectives simultaneously:

- We can save Social Security and its promises—without bankrupting the young.
- We can stimulate American growth and create new industries and high-paying jobs for our children. We can take the necessary steps to expand our economy, rather than fighting over who gets what from a dwindling pie.

- We can create **100 million** millionaires, and make every American a shareholder in a brighter future.

Here's how you can get off that economic treadmill I talked about in Chapter 4. Create a new two-tier Social Security and establish a mandated savings plan using existing tax dollars.

TIER 1

As we have seen, Social Security is now administered on a pay-as-you-go basis. Current employees pay money into Social Security and retired employees—yesterday's workers—receive the money. In the system I propose, the greater part of Social Security will remain pay-as-you-go, and this will be Tier 1. Everyone remains protected under the Tier 1, tax-based system, which acts as a safety net.

TIER 2

Under Tier 2, as you know from earlier discussion, you will be allowed to set aside money you are already paying into Social Security. Your set-aside will be deposited into a funded personal investment and retirement account through the new and independent corporation described below. Recall that anyone who pays at least $500 per year into Social Security will participate and that set-asides can range from $500 to $3,000 per year.

To save Social Security and to create the private investment to stimulate American economic growth, participation will be mandatory. At its best, the new system gives everyone the opportunity to become a shareholder in America's future. Even at its least successful, everyone receives Safety Net benefits under Tier 1.

Current Social Security promises families a floor of protection against poverty.

♦

The proposed funded Social Security system honors this promise by retaining the Tier 1 safety net guarantee.

More than 100 million Americans pay over $500 per year into Social Security. These Americans represent 80 percent of the total workforce. In the first year, the combined Tier 2 set-asides will invest $111.5 billion in savings; by the forty-fifth year, Tier 2 will invest over $200 billion in annual savings.

The Tier 2 system will begin immediately and will be phased in over a forty-five- to fifty-year period—one working lifetime. As an example, if we begin in the late 1990s, by the year 2013, when Social Security payments are expected to exceed revenues for the first time, all new retirees will have a substantial Social Security investment and retirement account to assist in the payment of Social Security. Part of Social Security benefits will come from Tier 1, pay-as-you-go taxes, part from income from the funded personal accounts. This will reduce the burden on current workers, yet will increase the amount available to retirees.

As each year goes by, the savings in the Social Security investment and retirement accounts will grow through compound interest and return on investment. As this growth occurs, the annual tax demands to cover the promised Social Security benefits will begin to decrease.

The goal is to save Social Security and assure its solvency for all Americans. Please see Chapter 11 "A Step-by-Step Plan," which analyzes how we can afford to pay for existing retirees under the old pay-as-you-go system while simultaneously implementing the new Tier 2 funded system.

Grow America   With all Social Security tax payments mandatory, just as they are today, your payroll taxes will continue to be paid to the Social Security Administration.

A portion of your taxes will be used by Social Security to pay the benefits to existing retirees. But another portion of your taxes, along with your voluntary savings match, will be sent to a newly formed and independent private-public entity—the Grow America Corporation—established by the president and the Congress, and will be deposited in the personal savings and retirement account you have chosen.

The Congress and Social Security will set up regulatory parameters for this corporation, and Grow America will then establish day-to-day, detailed operating rules to ensure that the monies remain available for retirement-only income and to foster responsible investment practices.

Grow America will need to establish "prudent person" investment guidelines to ensure that the private sector financial managers do not speculate in excessively high-risk investments. There will be no government guarantees of a specific rate of return on the funded investments.

The Grow America board of directors will comprise nine to eleven individuals nominated by the president and approved by the U.S. Senate. The Social Security administrator will sit on the board; but the majority of the board will be private sector representatives.

Grow America will license and approve responsible private sector financial managers, and the private sector will manage your personal account. From the list of approved private sector investment firms, you will be able to select the financial manager of your choice—a firm *that you choose,* from those certified for this purpose, will manage your money. You'll know it is your money, because you'll get regular financial statements, and you can watch your money grow. At any time, at no cost, you will be able to switch financial managers. The Tier 2 money will all be credited to individuals' personal accounts.

The ultimate success of this corporation is dependent on the clear public knowledge that the government does not control the investment policies or decisions over the money. Grow America will enable citizens to make self-governing choices for their future financial security.

Individual Americans will want to know that their money cannot be tampered with by government or political forces, and that their money is being invested wisely. The Grow America Corporation will establish

THE SYSTEM WILL ENABLE YOU TO BE SELF-GOVERNING

The Government and Grow America will
- develop trust
- set rules
- evaluate and certify asset managers
- provide information

◆

YOU will
- look at alternatives
- choose
- monitor
- change

◆

Asset managers will
- administer accounts

the proper criteria and review procedure to select professional financial managers to invest the money. The criteria will include the following central elements:

- a proven investment track record
- a minimum entry level in terms of the size of the total portfolio under management
- a minimum number of existing clients
- a thorough review and background check on the management and the principals

We are fortunate to have existing precedents in the private and public sectors to help design these selection criteria and procedures. There are existing large-scale systems—involving billions of dollars—for state, local, and corporate pensions. These can be used to create the appropriate structure. Other models of success, such as the system implemented in Chile, can also provide guidance.

The private sector financial managers will be expected to diversify investments and to seek a maximum, prudent rate of return for all participants. The mandate for these custodians is to utilize their best professional skills to protect and increase the assets under management.

Shareholder Oversight Panels

Washington is not the only power center that many Americans distrust. Average citizens may have had little experience with the investment community and are likely to distrust "Wall Street" as much as they distrust politicians. Many popular images of Wall Street are negative: illegal insider trading, brokers on commission "churning" accounts and gouging unsuspecting small investors, undertrained sales people forced to meet quotas on certain stock issues regardless of their underlying value or profit potential.

Investing $100 billion to $200 billion of annual savings will create huge investment portfolios. Simple, inexpensive oversight mechanisms can be established to build integrity and confidence into the system. The investment community should convene a council of blue chip leaders, whose integrity is beyond reproof, to recommend procedures and rules that will build grassroots confidence. These leaders will be at the forefront in designing a system that will benefit all Americans as shareholders. Yes, the system will foster competition and profitability, but the overriding concern needs to be for integrity and shareholder protection.

At very small cost, management firms could be required to establish a shareholder oversight panel for each fund. These panels could be modeled on the jury system: panels of twelve persons could be selected at random from the investors participating in each fund. The panelists could be trained by an independent organization to watch for potential abuses, and shareholder statements could include the panel's verification of compliance. The selected shareholders could serve for one or two years; then new panelists would be selected and trained.

The Safety Net   I have previously established that with the existence of the Tier 1 payroll-tax-supported system and the Tier 2 funded accounts, Social Security benefits will be paid from two sources. The Tier 1 system will remain as a safety net. When 5 percent of the income from your personal account does not equal Social Security Safety Net benefits, Tier 1 payroll taxes will make up the difference. In all cases where the 5 percent income from your capital account exceeds the Safety Net benefit level, you will retain all the surplus income. Again, all current beneficiaries will remain protected.

INDIVIDUAL PARTICIPATION

The following are the proposed conditions of participation:

1. Social Security will establish the mandatory two-tier system nationwide.

2. A fully operating funded system will accept *all* payments, and the $500 minimum will disappear.

3. Safety Net levels will be based on revenue available at the current 12.4 percent payroll tax rate, with no tax increases. You will receive benefits from the Tier 1 system to make up the difference if investments in your Tier 2 funded account do not produce income at this level.

4. The first $500 you pay into Social Security will go into your personal account. To keep up with inflation and real wage growth, the set-aside will increase by an estimated 5 percent per year. This keeps the set-aside at a constant percentage of wages.

5. To encourage national savings, Social Security will allow you, at your discretion, to increase your annual set-asides for your retirement

growth accounts. You will have opportunities to increase the set-aside based on a savings match that you provide voluntarily. This will occur on a sliding scale—for example:

- To raise your annual set-aside to $2,500 per year from $1,560, Social Security will add $1 of taxes you are already paying for every $2 of your savings match. Social Security will add $314 from your tax payments, and you will add about $12 per week, or $626 per year, for a total increase of $940. Your original $1,560 plus $940 equals $2,500.
- To raise your annual set-aside to the maximum $3,000 per year, $1,500 of taxes you are already paying will be combined with a dollar-for-dollar personal savings match of $1,500.

The benefit to you is substantial. You will be creating a nest egg which is growing tax-free to provide for your retirement; and, according to the proposal in this book, you will be able to pass the capital asset tax-free to your heirs. The benefit to the country is that you are increasing net savings and investment.

6. Consistent with increased life expectancy, normal retirement age (NRA) will rise to seventy. This can occur at a rate of two months per year beginning in 2011, and can be phased in gradually over an eighteen-year period. (As an example, each year, the NRA will go up two months. After six years, the NRA can rise one year.) Individuals will still be able to choose early retirement at sixty-two or sixty-five. Currently the NRA is being raised to sixty-six. This phasing-in will be completed by 2005. Senator Robert Kerrey and Senator Alan Simpson recommend that raising the NRA be continuous at two months per year until the NRA of seventy is reached by 2029.

Social Security is indexed for inflation and for cost-of-living adjustments (COLAs). Economists are concerned that actual inflation is lower than Social Security's indexing for inflation. Social Security benefits should remain indexed for inflation, but adjustments might be appropriate. Social Security is indexed again for real wages. The second recommendation is to raise real wage indexing at half of 1 percent per year as compared with 1 percent.

7. A goal of the Tier 2 funded system is to accumulate individual and national savings. Upon retirement, specific criteria will be applied

to oversee draw-downs of income and capital from personal accounts. So that the monies will be safeguarded for retirement use only, there must be some provision against retirees taking excessive amounts out of their accounts.

You will be able to opt for an annuity plan, based on life expectancy, with a view to depleting all assets by the time of your death, or the death of your spouse. But a preferred option is to retain the capital base and to be able to pass the capital on to your heirs tax-free. This will require a change in the tax law, but will allow future Americans, our children, to save their standard of living by having two sources of income.

Under this option, you (and your spouse) will live on the income from your capital during your retirement years and then pass the

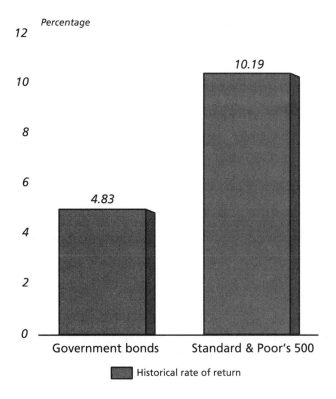

Rate of Return, 1926 to Present

Percentage

Government bonds: 4.83
Standard & Poor's 500: 10.19

Historical rate of return

Source: Ibbotson Associates, "Stocks, Bonds, Bills and Inflation," 1992 Yearbook: Market Results for 1926–1991 (Chicago, 1993).

remaining principal on to your heirs tax-free—up to $500,000 each (today's value). By taking only 5 percent income per year, you will preserve the capital base. This income will be offset against promised Tier 1 1995 benefits, dollar for dollar.

Individuals can expect retirement income to surpass promised Social Security benefits once the Tier 2 system matures. As related earlier, the Standard and Poor's 500 has returned 10.19 percent per year over the past seventy years. This compares favorably with government bonds— with a 4.83 percent return on long-term, and 5.09 percent intermediate.

Participation Incentives

In summary, all Americans will have the opportunity to become substantial capital owners. As the funded accounts grow, income for retirement will very often surpass current promised levels.

There will be an incentive in the funded system to retire at a later age. With compound interest, the value of the investment accounts increases dramatically between the forty-fifth and fiftieth years. Individuals who work from age twenty through seventy receive the benefit of the increased capital accumulation. For example, individuals who set aside $1,560 per year for forty-five years are projected to have $1,291,433 in their accounts. In the last five years alone, these accounts are projected to grow $714,366 to $2,005,799. Many will decide it's worth the wait.

Individuals who set aside $3,000 per year for forty-five years will have $2,483,526 in their accounts. After fifty years, they can expect $3,857,305—a $1,373,779 increase in the last five years.

Once workers begin to see the capital accumulating in their personal accounts, there will be an incentive to add to the voluntary personal savings matches—maybe $100, $150, or $200 per year. The models and examples I have used throughout this book assume that individuals work from age twenty to sixty-five—forty-five uninterrupted years. These illustrations offer easy-to-understand profiles, and offer highly representative indications of end results.

Social Security Administration records indicate, however, that these may not be normal workers. For example, 70 percent of males and females work before age twenty. Earnings in these years are usually low, but the 12.4 percent payroll taxes compounded for the extra time period will grow very substantially in personal savings and investment accounts.

Moreover, 30 percent of males and 20 percent of females work at ages sixty-five to sixty-nine. Nineteen percent of males and 8.5 percent of females work at ages seventy to seventy-nine. The effect of compounding set-aside money for an extra five to ten—or even fifteen—years will lead to a substantial increase in accumulated capital. Social Security records also indicate that even though work patterns are spread out over many more years, the average male works a total of 43.5 years, and the average female works an average of 41.0 years—less than the forty-five years assumed to define a working lifetime.

For a detailed discussion of Tier 2 benefits, please see the Appendix, where I show capital accumulations and Social Security benefits for the wage and salary workers participating in the plan. Capital accumulations for average real-life workers end up being 4.5 percent higher than the amount assumed for forty-five-year, age-twenty to -sixty-five average workers.

Has This Ever Worked Before?

W hat I am proposing in this book is a revolutionary plan for the U.S. Social Security system and the way Americans contribute to their private pension programs. Naturally, there will be some skepticism and some doubts. Some might ask: Has anything like this ever been tried before? Fair question. Putting the power of compound interest and the private sector to work to save Social Security is not an academic exercise. Working models, in which individuals have personal savings and retirement accounts, already exist in the real world.

These include two different foreign models—one in Chile and the other in Singapore—and one home-grown American variety.

WORKING MODELS OF REFORMED SYSTEMS

Chile   The best model in the world for a funded Social Security system is the plan used in Chile. In 1924, Chile was the first country in the Western Hemisphere to introduce a state-based social security system—later followed by the United States in 1935. In 1981, Chile set the leadership pace again by creating a funded system.

Under the funded system, 10 percent is set aside from every individual wage earner's paycheck, and these monies are deposited in an individual retirement account. The monies are professionally managed by the private sector operating competitively in the free market under government regulation. Individuals, without any penalties, can switch their monies from one manager to the next, based on performance and rate of return. The government ensures individuals a minimum social security benefit if the private funds fail.

Dr. José Piñera served as the chief architect of the Chilean system. A Harvard-trained economist, Dr. Piñera was Chile's minister of labor and social welfare in charge of implementation. At Dr. Piñera's insistence, the new system began on Labor Day—May 1, 1981. As he explains,

> May 1 has always been celebrated all over the world as a day of class confrontation, as a day when workers in a way fight the employers, as if their interests were completely divergent. When my view is that in a free-market economy, in a free society, their interests precisely are convergent. . . . We made every worker a capitalist, and there is no more powerful way, in my view, to stabilize a free-market economy and to get the consent, the approval of the workers of the country than to get them linked in a direct way to the benefits of the market economy.

Dr. Piñera emphasizes the change in attitude in the Chilean worker:

> Ninety percent of the workers chose the new system. Workers moved from the old system [the old pay-as-you-go system] to the new one faster than Germans going from Eastern Europe to Western Europe after the fall of the Berlin Wall. . . . Every Chilean worker goes around knowing that he has an individual pension account. More so, we have calculated that the main asset of the typical Chilean worker is not his small house or his used car, but the amount of capital that he has in his pension account.

Today, the Chilean pension assets exceed $20 billion. The International Center for Pension Reform, an independent, nonprofit policy organization based in Santiago, is seeking to promote the funding of state-run social security systems. The center points out that $20 billion in Chile is a huge pool of capital for a developing country of 13 million people and a GDP of $40 billion.

The mechanics of the Chilean system are worth exploring. Some of the highlights include the following:

- Each month **10** percent of workers' wages are deposited in the individual investment accounts. The goal is for workers to have a pension fund at retirement equal to **70** percent of their final salary.
- A worker selects any one of twenty existing private sector Pension Fund Administration companies (Administradoras de Fondos de Pensiones—AFPs) in which to invest the savings.

- The government has strict regulation policies to control the types of allowable investments and the overall makeup of the portfolios. The specific purpose is to benefit from higher private sector rates of return—without allowing excessive risk taking or overconcentration of assets. Regulation is important to keep out high-roller investments such as junk bonds, and to prevent future "Orange County" fiascoes.
- A worker may contribute a voluntary savings deposit up to an additional **10** percent of wages.
- People can use a computer in the storefront branch offices of many AFPs to calculate the amount of money they wish to have in their account when they retire and the age at which they wish to retire. They can check their balances and adjust their monthly contribution levels to meet their goals.
- Pay-as-you-go systems can discriminate against the low-income worker. Very often, low-income workers begin work early, work many years, pay into the system throughout those years, and then die early. They do not receive their hard-earned benefits. *Under a funded system, their savings are theirs and can be passed on to their children.*
- An additional **3** percent of wage is set aside for group life and disability insurance.

Dr. Piñera stresses two central issues when discussing the Chilean system. First, pay-as-you-go social security systems around the world are facing very serious solvency problems as populations age. Fewer workers are burdened with paying for an increasing number of beneficiaries, which creates major tension between generations. In Dr. Piñera's words, "The facts that the birth rate is going down and that life expectancy is increasing mean that in the twenty-first century, whatever the good intentions of the creators of the pay-as-you-go systems, those systems will have enormous financial problems."

Second, Dr. Piñera feels that people thrive when they own their money, and are happy about taking charge of their own retirement. The Chilean system is based on a fundamental belief in individual rights and the freedom to control your own destiny. Dr. Piñera sums this up: "Workers, who have an intuitive knowledge of whatever is close to their lives, like pension, education and health, are able to choose in the right direction, I do believe; that's why I do believe so much in their freedom to choose."

Chile serves as the model for Latin America. Argentina, Peru, and Colombia are following the Chilean example and have created new, funded social security systems. Others—Bolivia and Brazil—are in the process of reform. Mexico is introducing a modest capitalized system.

Singapore

Singapore uses the power of government to create a nationwide institutionalized savings plan for all wage earners—a provident fund model. In 1955 the parliament of Singapore created the Central Provident Fund (CPF). The employer and employee pay equal shares.

In 1995, the employer and employee share was 5 percent of wage (total 10 percent) up to a maximum taxable wage level of $6,000. By 1991, mandated savings had risen to 40 percent—22.5 percent coming from the employee's wage and 17.5 percent coming from the employer— up to a maximum taxable wage of $72,000 (the equivalent of $40,000 in the United States).

The plan covers more than 2 million workers, representing three-fourths of the workforce. The self-employed are not covered. The plan began as a mandated savings plan for retirement only. Beginning in 1968, CPF expanded its allowable uses to include most conventional family savings needs: home ownership, education, and "Medisave Accounts" to cover hospitalization. By year end 1989, the distribution of withdrawals from savings broke down into the following categories by percentage:

Home ownership	66 percent
Retirement	17 percent
Medisave	5 percent
Other	12 percent

As the participating membership grows older and retires, the monies spent on retirement and hospitalization will increase.

Each CPF member has three accounts—an ordinary account, a Medisave account, and a special account. The ordinary account can be used for home ownership, the Medisave account for hospitalization, and the special account for retirement. The government determines allowed allocations for each account by percent of wage.

The government controls the investment of the savings, and offers the members an established tax-free interest rate. The employees have title to the money accumulating in their accounts. On their death, they may pass these monies on tax-free to their heirs.

The Singapore provident fund model is used by countries in Southeast Asia, including Malaysia. It must be said that the Singapore model is based on very strong government planning, management, and regulation—a centralized approach that is contrary to the concept of America's freedoms and self-governance tradition of individual choice. The irony, however, is that America, under our existing government tax and spend, pay-as-you-go systems, is transferring more and more of our financial resources into federal hands and federal management.

The 40 percent Singapore tax rate for savings is initially shocking. But that's where we are headed, ourselves, with our projected payroll taxes of 25.69 percent by 2030 (17.22 percent for Social Security and 8.46 percent for Medicare Part A [HI]). Medicare Part B (SMI) comes out of general tax revenues. The cost of SMI is the equivalent of another 8 to 9 percent of payroll. The total is approaching 35 percent of all wages. The difference between the Singapore mandated savings percentage and the projected percentage of U.S. payroll taxes is even less when we consider that a major part of Singapore's savings is for home ownership—not included in the American numbers.

The American Pension System   The private and local government pension systems in America offer valuable models demonstrating the advantages of putting private sector investment to work to benefit retirees. Of the $4.2 trillion capital in the pension system, much of the capital is invested in corporate stocks and equities. The rate of return on these private and public investments outperform investments in government bonds—generating substantially higher retirement benefits for participants. (It is striking that public pension funds at the sub-federal level have performed as well as have private funds. Therefore, the disparity is not simply a matter of "public vs. private.")

Peter Drucker, in *The Unseen Revolution,* credits Charles Wilson, the CEO of General Motors in 1950, with developing and implementing the model for modern private pensions. There are two central elements to Wilson's system-changing approach. The most important is to invest pension assets in the productive capital markets. Prior to the Wilson and General Motors innovations, most pension assets were invested in government bonds. Wilson argued that investing pension assets in the private sector would help American economic growth and benefit the retiree because of the multiplier effect of compound interest. The capital growth and rate of return over the past fifty years in private sector and government pensions offer strong evidence that Social Security beneficiaries and economic development are being seriously short-changed by not having a two-tier Social Security system. Setting aside billions of dollars each year into funded personal accounts within the Social Security system assuredly will provide retirees with increased benefits and will help in the economic revitalization of the United States.

The second element in Wilson's plan was to assure that pension funds be managed by independent, professional managers. He wanted to assure that the employer or governmental body did not use the large pools of capital for its own self-serving ends. Based on the current track record of the United States government in managing the Social Security Trust Fund, Wilson has proved to be prophetic. What independent professional would allow the government to appropriate every penny of the assets of the trust fund to cover the government's runaway spending? What independent professional would choose to invest 100 percent of the $475 billion trust fund in federal bonds, and not a penny in corporate and equity growth stocks?

PRACTICAL BENEFITS

Over the next few years, we can expect heated, nonstop debates on Social Security, entitlements, and balancing the budget. The final result will include trade-offs in taxation, benefits, retirement age, and the delivery of medical services.

As we saw at the end of Chapter 5, we all face a vital choice in America. We can see our economy as a fixed entity. In this case lines will be drawn, and there will be fights over limited assets. The other option is a vision of an expanding America with similarly expanding opportunity for all. The basis of this possibility is to increase savings and investment and to invite all Americans to be shareholders in a brighter future.

The creation of a two-tier Social Security system is the most concrete and immediately practical solution, and will become the cornerstone to the new approach. Nineteen ninety-seven will be a critical year. After the 1996 presidential election there will be a three- to five-year window of opportunity for reform. All experts agree that the current system is in jeopardy. Postponing a decision until 2013, when the Social Security deficits begin, will multiply the problems and will multiply the costs. By 2013 we will no longer be able to afford the transition. Watch 1997.

There are four major benefits to funding part of Social Security through individual investment and retirement accounts:

1. Ownership   Eighty percent of working Americans can participate. Over 100 million Americans will become substantial capital owners and shareholders. The tangible capital ownership by over 100 million working men and women will transform economic opportunity in America.

2. Credibility   There is serious frustration among young workers. They are currently paying 12.4 percent of their wages into a system they don't believe in and from which they expect no benefits. They don't believe in it because they know that none of their money is being set aside for their future. But if they could set their current tax payments aside in investment and retirement accounts, they would have substantial capital assets to cover their retirement. The creation of the Tier 2 funded system will go a long way to restore the belief of young Americans in the security of their future retirement.

3. The Potential for Increased Retirement Benefits   The figure "Rate of Return, 1926 to Present," in Chapter 7, shows the return on investment and underlines the potential for increasing the benefits paid to the elderly in retirement.

Returns on private sector investments are not guaranteed. There is a risk. But the likelihood, as I have shown elsewhere, is that retirement benefits would increase for 80 to 100 million Americans once the system matures. In future years, as the tax demands on the Tier 1, pay-as-you-go system decrease, the allowable set-asides in the Tier 2 funded system can double—all within the parameters of existing payroll taxes.

The rules in the proposed Social Security funded system will be clear and strict: No withdrawals of monies for any purposes other than retirement should be permitted. Upon retirement, clear rules will govern the use of the capital base. Individuals should have the right to create an annuity so that they receive payments until their death, or the death of their spouses—including the consumption of all the principal if they wish. Or they should have the right to live off the interest or equity growth and pass the remaining principal, tax-free, to their heirs.

4. An Expanded Economy

An extra $100 billion to $200 billion per year of savings invested in the private sector will expand the economy.

Economic growth depends on net new savings (see Chapter 14 for a more detailed discussion). In a 1988 book, *Can America Afford to Grow Old?* three respected economists, Henry Aaron, Barry Bosworth, and Gary Burtless, carefully studied the economic impact of investing the Social Security surpluses that were then expected from 1988 to 2020 in the private economy. Their economic model assumed that non–Social Security federal deficits would be restrained at 1.5 percent of Gross National Product (GNP). At these levels the results of their analysis were very favorable in terms of new jobs created, new industries financed, and overall economic growth. They predicted that the added savings and capital investment would lead to higher real wages, an expanding GNP and a more competitive America:

> Our results indicate that the added future consumption that results
> from saving and investing today's Social Security surplus is more
> than enough to offset all of the increased burden on future workers
> of providing pensions for a larger population of retirees. The
> benefits of this policy in the form of increased wages and
> consumption, made possible by a larger capital stock, exceed the
> added costs of Social Security benefit payments.

Wall Street and Capitol Hill, Republicans and Democrats agree that added savings lead to added capital investment and future economic growth.

Make the Private Pension System
Fit the Modern Workplace

In preparing to write this book, as I've mentioned previously, I convened a series of focus groups. The participants were amazed by how little they knew about finance, capital, and their pensions. Many were sophisticated accountants, lawyers, and small business owners. And yet, they were startled to realize how uneducated most of us are about economics and money.

Very few people—almost no one—had a focus on their largest potential asset, their pension. For the most part they couldn't answer the two most basic questions: Is your pension money yours; do you own the capital? And how much will you get when you retire; are you sure? In fact, existing pension tax laws have the potential to unlock opportunity for all Americans, to allow us all to have a stake in the economy, and accumulate wealth. In a free market economy, each of us can become a capitalist.

Dallas Salisbury is president of the nonpartisan Employee Benefit Research Institute (EBRI) in Washington, D.C., the nation's leading pension education organization. Salisbury's background is finance and accounting. Commenting on the potential of pensions to extend capital ownership to everyone, he says, "I've been at EBRI since our beginning in 1978. My friends can't understand why I've stayed here so long. The answer is that pensions offer individuals their best chance to increase savings and accumulate capital, and pensions offer America our best chance for economic growth and international competitiveness. This is a very exciting place to work."

WHAT DO YOU KNOW ABOUT YOUR PENSION?

The security of your pension, the funding levels of your pension, your vesting and portability rights, and your investment performance are all critical to your economic security in your senior years. You work all your life and you "think" you have a good pension. Do you really know what to expect?

If your pension has the potential of being your largest capital asset— up to ten times the value of owning a home—what do you know about your pension? If you don't have a pension, ask yourself, Why not? Find out why your standard of living for the last third of your life—after retirement—is at risk. Find out how you are missing an important opportunity to accumulate wealth.

Your employer is paying money into your pension. Often you are matching this money. Is the money yours? The laws and tax incentives exist now to enable millions of Americans to become substantial capital owners through their pensions. How does *your* pension work?

Before you read on, please answer the Pension Questionnaire.

A COMPARISON: WHAT DO YOU KNOW ABOUT YOUR HOME?

Home ownership is a source of great pride. There are more homeowners in America than in any other nation. All homeowners have a stake in America, in their community, in their neighborhood. If you are a home-owner, answer the Home Ownership Questionnaire on page 114. Then check and see which you know more about, your home or your pension, and ask yourself why.

In the pension focus groups, I found that homeowners were very knowledgeable about the financial aspects of their home. They knew how much they had paid, the current estimated value, total mortgage, interest rates, and monthly payments.

The participants were startled to find how little they knew about their pensions compared with how much they knew about their homes. And they were provoked. As a result of the discussion about pensions, they realized how important the pension issue is to their future standard of living and to accumulating wealth. Then they were mad at themselves for knowing so little, and often mad at their employer for offering so little information or guidance. Most, when they asked their employers about their pensions, felt that the answers were vague and confusing.

Pension Questionnaire

1. Do you have any kind of pension coverage?

   Yes _____ No _____
   Don't know _____

2. How much money is in your pension now?

   $ _____
   Don't know _____

3. Do you receive periodic statements telling you how much money is in your pension?

   Yes _____ No _____
   Don't know _____

4. Is the money yours? Do you own the capital?

   Yes _____ No _____
   Don't know _____

5. When you retire, how much money will you receive each year?
   What percentage of your salary?

   $ _____
   Don't know _____
   _____ %

6. Do you know the ways your employer can terminate your pension benefits?

   Yes _____ No _____
   Don't know _____

7. Can you change jobs and take your accumulated pension money with you? Or do you lose it?

   Can take it _____
   Lose it _____
   Don't know _____

8. Who controls and manages your pension money?
   What annual rate of return are you getting on your money?
   If you are not satisfied with the management of your money, can you switch money managers?

   Name _____
   Don't know _____
   _____ % return/year
   Don't know _____
   Yes _____ No _____
   Don't know _____

9. What are the total administrative costs related to managing your money? What service fees and money management fees are charged against you?

   $ _____ per year
   Don't know _____
   $ _____ per year
   Don't know _____

10. Is your pension fully funded?

    Yes _____ No _____

11. Does your employer make regular contributions to your pension?

    Yes _____ No _____
    Don't know _____

Or does your employer promise to pay "sometime" in the future?

Yes _____ No _____

Don't know _____

11. When you reach retirement age, what will the total estimated value (capital value) of your pension be?

$ _____

Don't know _____

12. If you die, will your spouse receive this money?

Yes _____ No _____

Don't know _____

13. When you and your spouse die, what happens to your money?

Answer: _____

_____

Can you give the money to your children?

Yes _____ No _____

Don't know _____

What are the estate taxes?

_____ % $ _____

Don't know _____

What are the income taxes?

_____ % $ _____

Don't know _____

How much money will your children really receive after tax?

$ _____

Don't know _____

Home Ownership Questionnaire

If you own your home:

1. What did you pay for your house?

$ _____

2. What is the estimated value of your house today?

$ _____

3. Do you have a mortgage?

Yes _____ No _____

4. How big is your mortgage?

$ _____

5. What are your monthly payments?

$ _____

6. What annual interest rate are you paying?

_____ %

7. What is the term of your loan? How many years?

_____

Are You Satisfied with Your Pension Knowledge?

Test yourself. After you completed the pension questionnaire, were you:

Happy with your answers?	Yes _____ No _____
Certain of your knowledge?	Yes _____ No _____
Confused?	Yes _____ No _____
Angry?	Yes _____ No _____

PENSION POWER

Becoming a millionaire through the pension system sounds simple, and it is. But there are conditions.

Tax Advantages   First, it is essential to understand the difference between regular savings, and "savings" inside a pension vehicle. Regular savings are taxed twice by the federal government. You earn income, and your income is taxed. You earn $100, and the government takes $20 to $30 in taxes—leaving $70 to $80 in your savings account. As the money earns interest and grows, the federal government taxes the growth. For every $100 of interest or growth in your money, the government takes a second $20 to $30 in taxes. In regular savings, you are saving after-tax dollars, and your interest, the growth of your money, is being taxed.

In pensions, your "savings" go into your account tax-free, and the interest earned, the growth of your money, is tax-free. In pensions, almost twice the money is at work for you as in an ordinary savings account. Pensions offer very significant tax advantages. Through already existing federal tax incentives, employers can set money aside for you into a pension—tax-free. You can help match it—tax-free. As your money makes money and grows, the growth accumulates—tax-free.

These tax benefits are one of the two key devices, together with compound interest, to make you a millionaire.

Professional Management   Second, professional financial management is vital to attain the necessary and reasonable rate of return on the money we invest. When we have a health problem, we go to a doctor—a professional. We don't try to diagnose, prescribe medicine, or operate on ourselves. We consult with doctors who are specially trained and spend all their lives in medicine. Financial management is the same. Asset managers are also specially trained, and they spend their lives analyzing and looking for the best investment opportunities to get the highest rate of return.

The difference between using professional investment management and doing it yourself is likely to be substantial. To make the point, let's select two extremes. One individual buys long-term government bonds. The second individual hires a professional financial manager and invests in corporate equities. Remember that over the past seventy years, the rate of return on government long-term bonds has averaged 4.8 percent, whereas the rate of return on the Standard and Poor's 500 corporate equities has been 10.19 percent.

For forty-five years, each investor sets aside $30 every week increased 5 percent per year for inflation and real wage growth. Assume that one receives a 6 percent return on investment and the other a 10 percent return. What is the end result? At a 6 percent rate of return, the end result is $783,909. At a 10 percent rate of return, the end result is $2,241,120. The individual who hired the financial manager has $1,457,211 *more* from his or her investments!

All of us can learn from the rich. Wealthy individuals almost always use professional asset management, and they expect a 10 to 12 percent return on their investments. If they don't get the expected return, they change managers. In sports—baseball, football, and hockey—losing teams change managers. The same is true with financial management. If the rich expect a 10 to 12 percent return on their money and use professional asset managers, why should *we* accept a 6 percent return?

Discipline   Third, to become a millionaire, you need to set money aside throughout your working career—without interruption. You need patience and discipline. But can you catch up if you start in your late thirties or early forties?

- Between you and your employer, you must set aside **$25** to **$30** every week—for forty-five to fifty years.
- As the money grows, you can't touch it.

STARTING A PENSION AT AGE THIRTY OR FORTY: CAN YOU CATCH UP?

Begin at age thirty—at an 8 percent return:

- Set aside **$30** a week for thirty years, you can accumulate **$516,670**.
- Set aside **$30** a week for forty years, you can accumulate **$822,604**.

◆

Begin at age forty—at an 8 percent return:

- Set aside **$30** a week for twenty-five years, you can accumulate **$191,155**.
- Set aside **$60** a week for thirty years, you can accumulate **$636,890**.

◆

These figures assume a 5 percent set-aside increase per year.

Many people in their twenties and early thirties don't save. They only begin to think of savings in their mid- to late thirties or forties, and they may then be discouraged because it is so late. But it is never too late to start. Begin at age thirty or age forty, or anywhere in between. The multipliers are not as great if you shorten the time period, but your earning power is probably greater than it was when you were younger. You might be able to make up the difference by setting more money aside. If you can set aside $30 a week, $50 a week, $75 a week, or even $100 a week, the result is still substantial. Even if you didn't start at the outset of your working life, you can go a long way to make your senior years economically more secure.

In summary, the pension system offers you a substantial opportunity to set aside tax-free money to achieve economic security for your senior years, and to become a substantial capital owner—all in one working lifetime.

A QUIET REVOLUTION

In the past forty years there has been a quiet revolution in American pensions. Almost everyone has been caught by surprise, and it might take twenty to thirty years of education about pensions to bring our general knowledge to the proper level.

Even the experts dealing with pension issues day-to-day have been dazzled. In 1950, the total pension assets held in the United States were $25 billion. In 1990, just forty years later, the total pension assets were $4.2 trillion. In 1950, 10 million Americans participated in pensions. Today, 51 million Americans have some pension coverage.

The capital pool amassed in American pensions can best be described as staggering. Financial analysts and other inside technicians have seen it, but even they have been amazed by the scale of the change and its impact in the financial markets. The average American remains unaware of this huge economic force.

Moreover, even though capital in pensions now exceeds $4.2 trillion, we are still early on the growth curve. Pension assets will soon surpass the GDP, which stood at $6.9 trillion at year end 1994.

Besides the tremendous growth in pension assets, the second part of the quiet revolution is the change in types of pension plans. There are two basic types of pension plans: defined benefit and defined contribution.

Originally, most pensions were set up as defined benefit plans—both in the private sector and in government. Under defined benefit plans, the employer makes a commitment to pay you a *defined benefit*, an agreed-to amount of money every year after retirement until your death and usually the death of your spouse. The employee does not *own* a penny of the capital paid in by the employer. The employer funds the pension, manages the capital, and has an obligation to pay the money.

In recent years, however, more and more pensions have become defined contribution plans. There is a wide variety of defined contribution plans: Keogh plans, SEPs, ESOPs, and, most important, 401(k)s. Under defined contribution plans, *the pension money is yours*—you own the capital. The employer has no obligation to pay you a set sum of money after retirement. Your coverage depends on the amount of money in the fund when you retire. That amount of money is based on two factors: how much has been paid in over the years, and the accumulated capital growth.

Part of the broad-scale revolution is broad-scale confusion. Whose money is this? In defined contribution plans, the money belongs to the employee. In defined benefit plans the employer has one view, and most employees have another.

Defined Benefit Plans: The Employer's View

In the private sector, most pensions began as defined benefit plans. They were optional for the company and were created by employers on a voluntary basis. They were not seen as part of the employees' compensation, and employees had no right to the pension. Often they were designed by employers as an incentive to keep employees with a company long-term.

In the public sector, most pensions are also defined benefit plans. The beneficiaries were first police and firemen, then teachers. The pensions offered extra security to employees, and were part of the incentives attracting employees to government service.

In defined benefit plans, the obligation rests with the employers. Employers take their financial obligation to pay very seriously, and they are protective of their prerogatives. They don't encourage employees to be too inquisitive about the status of the money. The employee has a "pension claim" to an agreed-to income for life after retirement, but no ownership.

Defined Benefit Plans: The Employee's View

Research on employee viewpoints shows that most employees think the money in their defined benefit plan is theirs. They think their pension is part of their compensation.

Reality: Where's Your Money?

What is the reality? Fifty-one million Americans have some form of pension. This represents approximately 50 percent of the workforce, which leaves about 50 percent of the workforce with no pension. These individuals are heavily dependent on Social Security.

Defined contribution plans have been growing in number and asset value over the past twenty years. In 1976 only 13 percent of people with pensions had defined contribution plans as their primary plan, but this had risen to 32 percent by 1987. That is, as of 1987, 68 percent of individuals with pensions had defined benefit plans as their primary plan, and 32 percent had defined contribution plans as their primary plan. Still in 1991, 77 percent of pension assets were in defined benefit plans, compared with 23 percent in defined contribution plans.

Of the $4.2 trillion paid into the pension system, while individuals feel that the money paid in is theirs, less than 25 percent is actually owned by individuals. Where's your money?

Pension Problems in the Modern Workplace

Modern workers will have three or four different careers and six to ten jobs in their lifetimes. Most young workers starting out don't think about retirement and don't have pensions. Most small businesses don't offer pensions. In defined benefit pensions, most companies' vesting and portability rules cause workers to lose their money every time they change jobs.

In defined benefit plans, for the most part, as soon as you and your spouse die, your financial claim ends. As an example, if you and your spouse live to be ninety-five, and you retire at sixty-five, if your pension contract states that you will receive $25,000 per year for life, you will

The Goal: Pension Contributions for a Full Working Career with Immediate Vesting and Portability

IMMEDIATE VESTING AND PORTABILITY

A pension should be part of your compensation—with immediate vesting (your first payment into your pension comes with your first paycheck on every job) and portability (when you change jobs, you take the accumulated money with you). Begin at age twenty. Set aside $25 to $30 per week. When you retire, you'll be a millionaire.

receive thirty times $25,000, or $750,000. But if you and your spouse die after two years, you will receive $50,000. Even if the company paid in $3,000 per year for forty years and even if this money has grown eight times in the financial and equity markets to $960,000, you receive only the $50,000. Where's your money?

Most of the largest corporations in America have established defined benefit plans, very often these plans have been well managed. These plans are now reaching maturity, and the money being set aside is starting to show very substantial growth. If your pension were considered compensation, this money could be yours; but defined benefit plans are not structured that way. Any surplus capital growth stays in the pension and helps to meet future beneficiary claims. Where's your money?

The Future of Defined Benefits

The best measure of the capital accumulation is that 90 percent of the Fortune 500 company pensions are 160 percent funded, or more. Many of these companies are not putting any more money into their pension funds. Pension surpluses are viewed by the company as important corporate assets. The money paid in for you is now set aside to benefit your replacement.

It is not my purpose to deny that defined benefit plans play a very important role in the American pension system. To be economically secure during your senior years is vital, and being assured of receiving a decent income until your death and the death of your spouse goes a long way to assure your quality of life.

In Washington, pension professionals are debating the issue of defined benefit plans vs. defined contribution plans. The advocates of defined benefit plans view them as the only true pensions and denigrate defined contribution plans as "do-it-yourself" impostors. These advocates appreciate that the employers have taken on the responsibility of assuring a defined payment stream to the vested retirees and that, with professional management, these funds ensure decent income for the employees.

In Washington there is also great concern that defined contribution plans will not be professionally managed by the employees and that the rates of return will not be sufficient to provide the same economic security.

It is important, however, to be aware that pension vehicles exist through which you can own the money. You need to be aware of your alternatives and then, with professional assistance, prepare a retirement and pension plan best suited to your income level and personal goals. A preferred model might be to have both a defined benefit plan to offer you basic security and a defined contribution plan through which you can accumulate capital ownership.

A Pension System to Protect You: The TIAA-CREF Model

Immediate Vesting and Portability The Bureau of Labor Statistics reports that median tenure with the same employer was 4.5 years in January 1991. This leads to the conclusion, which I have reported earlier in this book, that an individual in the modern workplace can expect to hold six to ten jobs in one working lifetime.

In view of this expected job turnover frequency, any pension system that is truly to benefit employees must provide immediate vesting and portability. Current pension laws require five-year vesting (you may not be eligible for benefits until you've worked that long for the organization), which is more than the median job tenure. Moving your pension capital from one fund, or one employer, to the next is not easy. But we have seen that building substantial capital ownership requires individuals to begin the set-asides when they join the workforce, and continue the pay-ins without interruption during their working lifetimes.

The reality of the modern workplace requires a new pension model. The best real-world model is TIAA-CREF, the Teachers Insurance and Annuity Association–College Retirement Equities Fund, established by Andrew Carnegie in 1918 to benefit teachers and professors, although members of other professions can now participate. The TIAA-CREF model is important because the pension assets are owned by the individual employees—the teachers and other educational professionals. As money is paid into the pension, the participants receive statements showing how their individual accounts are growing.

The TIAA-CREF design responds to the mobility of the modern workplace, allowing employees to build substantial capital assets and an important income stream for retirement. The model includes the features described in the following sections.

Teachers Annuity (TIAA-CREF): A Model for the Modern Workplace

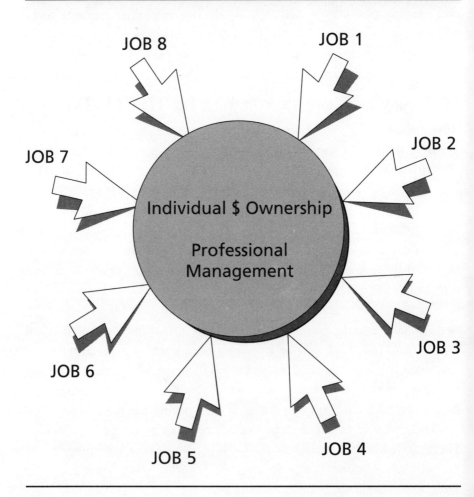

JOB 8   JOB 1

JOB 7

JOB 2

Individual $ Ownership

Professional Management

JOB 3

JOB 6

JOB 5   JOB 4

Individual Ownership and Individual Accounts

The participants individually own the capital assets in their pensions, and they receive regular individual reports on the value of their money. There is no credibility gap in this system.

Uninterrupted Coverage

Teachers negotiate their pension as part of their compensation. Their employer agrees to set aside a given amount of salary, and the employee has a choice whether or not to match part of it. These monies vest immediately and are paid monthly or biweekly to TIAA-CREF. To make the magic of compound interest work for you, immediate vesting is important, because the multipliers only work if the payments are received without major funding gaps. When an employee switches jobs, the next employer negotiates compensation with the employee, and makes the pension payments to TIAA-CREF without interruption. In this way, there is continuous coverage as the participant goes from one job to the next.

The Equivalent of Forced Savings

When employees make the decision to participate, the monthly or biweekly payments are automatic. The pension payments are the equivalent of forced savings. The same is true of a home mortgage or a business loan. Once individuals make the decision to participate, the monies are set aside. Once you sign a home mortgage with a bank, you don't review every month whether you wish to make the payment. There are so many demands on income that some type of contract or agreed-to payment schedule, voluntarily entered into, seems necessary to make the system function properly.

System Management

TIAA-CREF professionally manages the participants' assets in a central pool of capital similar to a mutual fund. The rate of return at TIAA-CREF exceeded 10 percent from 1982 through 1991.

The TIAA-CREF model lends itself to small businesses. The two major objections by small businesses to establishing a pension plan for their employees is that they can't afford the pension payments and that compliance with the federal Employee Retirement Income Security Act (ERISA) is very expensive and burdensome. They just don't want more government paperwork.

At no new cost, however, small businesses can establish a working relationship with a TIAA-CREF type of system. All the legal and administrative burdens are borne by the single pension entity, not the small business. The small businesses can participate in the set-asides, or the employees can participate on a voluntary basis without funding from the small business. Whether or not the small businesses and the employees participate depends on individual cost-benefit decisions.

The U.S. Department of Labor has an interesting analysis which offers some positive evidence that individuals will set money aside if they are properly informed. On the lower end of the economic scale, of the 19.7 million employees receiving less than $5 per hour, only 6.5 percent were offered a 401(k) pension plan. Of the 6.5 percent, 35 percent participated at some level. At $10 to $12.49 per hour wage, 34.3 percent of the 9.1 million employees were offered participation in a 401(k) plan, and 59.8 percent participated. These statistics are encouraging and indicate that sustained marketing and economic education combined with making appropriate investment vehicles available can lead to substantial results.

The TIAA-CREF-style systems can be offered to employees in small and large businesses, government, and the nonprofit sector with equal validity. Any employee not currently covered by a pension can benefit. Employees now covered by a defined benefit plan might wish on a voluntary basis to set additional income aside into a plan if they own the assets.

★ *10* ★

Let Your Money Make Money

I've said it before, but it is worth repeating: Savings, increased not only through our deposits but through the magic of compound interest, are the source of our economic future and security.

Every child growing up loves a magic show. The sleight of hand always amazes, and the creation of something beautiful—a rabbit or a bouquet of flowers—out of nothing never ceases to capture the imagination. To the adult that child becomes, the multiplier effect of compound interest has the same qualities. The return on investment based on compound interest is magical and amazing. After all, Albert Einstein was once asked, "What is the most powerful force on earth?" Without delay, the Nobel Prize-winning mathematician answered, "Compound interest."

The benefit of compound interest can—and should—work for you. Everyone has heard that money makes money. The only stumbling block is that people see this as a tool for the rich: "Money makes money" gets translated as "The rich get richer." In fact, all employed Americans can benefit from this principle. There is no real mystery to money making money, but let's examine how it works. Money earns interest from banks, the government, any borrower. In addition, you may invest in businesses (buy stocks) and the businesses may pay dividends; if the businesses do well and grow, the value of the stocks (your equity) goes up.

YOUR MONEY AT WORK

Repeatedly I have mentioned that individuals who set aside $25 to $30 a week for forty-five to fifty years will become millionaires. The reason, once again, is that compound interest is at work. Let's determine just how much your accumulated money makes for you each year. Assume that each year you and your employer invest $30 per week, or $1,560 per year in the fund. Assume an 8 percent compound rate of return. Based on expected inflation and real wage growth, include a 5 percent annual set-aside increase. Each year how much money is your money making for you? In the beginning the answer is, Not much. In Year 1, you invest $1,560, and a compound 8 percent rate of return nets you $64. But as the years go by, the money your money makes becomes more and more interesting:

- During Year 10, your money makes **$4,508** for you.
- During Year 20, your money makes **$12,119** for you.
- During Year 30, your money makes **$30,204** for you.
- During Year 40, your money makes **$72,125** for you.
- During Year 50, your money makes **$167,720** for you.

Think about it. This is more than enough to live on each year during your lifetime, without invading the principal. At your death, you can pass $1 million on to your children.

THE IMPORTANCE OF EARLY MONEY

Anyone aged twenty to thirty should focus on this vital fact: the most important money is the early money. To continue the example from the preceding section, after ten years you will have $28,888. This may not seem like much for retirement, and you could use it to buy a new car or a boat or redo the kitchen. But left in the fund, this money will double every eight years. Watch the multiplier.

Year 10	$28,888
Year 18	$57,776
Year 24	$115,552
Year 32	$231,104
Year 40	$462,208
Year 50	$924,416

If you start late try to catch up at the end, assume you invest more— up to $100 a week, or $5,200 a year for the last ten years of your employment. This is important to do, but your end result is $96,293. Thirty dollars a week for the *first* ten years nets you $924,160 after fifty years. One hundred dollars a week for the last ten years nets you $96,293.

The Power of Compound Interest

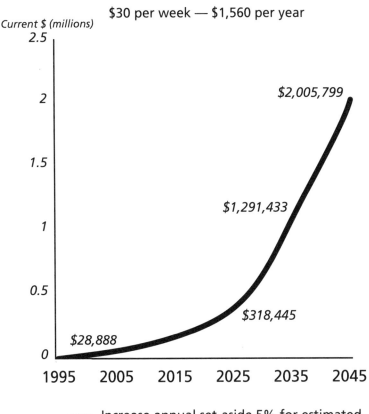

$30 per week — $1,560 per year

Current $ (millions)

$2,005,799

$1,291,433

$318,445

$28,888

1995   2005   2015   2025   2035   2045

━━ Increase annual set-aside 5% for estimated inflation and real wage growth

This analysis is very important for anyone who is twenty to thirty. At this age, you might not wish to focus on retirement or saving, but these years are vital.

HOW TO CREATE 100 MILLION MILLIONAIRES

The Nuts and Bolts of the Plan

A Step-by-Step Plan

The devil is in the details, they say. And I am offering a very specific plan for increasing our financial independence and security. Not every reader will want to know as much about the plan as this section of the book offers, but if this challenge to the status quo is to be taken seriously, it is critical that the nuts and bolts of the proposal be revealed.

This chapter recapitulates and sums up the Social Security and pension reforms that I have already proposed—and tells how we can afford the transition. The discussion is directed to especially curious general readers and to the experts. The details of reform can be refined and amended. But what is important, as I have emphasized, is launching a national debate on individual control, independence, acceptable levels of taxation, and the opportunity for all Americans to share in the rewards of our economic system.

Can one working generation afford to pay for two Social Security systems as we meet our obligations under the old system and set aside capital for the new system? We must continue to meet our promises to existing retirees under the Tier 1, pay-as-you-go system, and, at the same time, accumulate enough money under the Tier 2 funded system to capitalize more than 100 million personal investment and retirement accounts.

HOW TO AFFORD PERSONAL ACCOUNTS UNDER SOCIAL SECURITY IN ONE WORKING GENERATION

We can afford it. There are choices and trade-offs, but the arithmetic is favorable. Ironically, what we cannot afford to do is to continue Social Security as it is currently constituted, as a single-tier system in which the working generation pays the retirement benefits of the no-longer-working, retired generation—unless we enact substantial tax increases, which Americans don't want.

The existing system is expected to have annual surpluses from 1996 through 2012, averaging about $25 billion per year. The impact of the retiring baby boomers is not expected to show up until 2013, when, as we have seen in previous chapters, the deficits begin.

The underlying problem is simple: There are 44.5 million beneficiaries in 1996, and this number will rise to over 80 million in the year 2030—almost double in just thirty-five years.

The first year when the pay-as-you-go system is projected to exceed a $100 billion per year deficit is 2022. This builds to a $200 billion per year deficit in 2032, and rises to a $225.1 billion per year deficit in 2040, the end of forty-five years—the span of one working lifetime, cited frequently in this book. So after forty-five years—despite seventeen years of surpluses—the system will have spent $27.2 trillion dollars and will show a $4.1 trillion accumulated deficit.

This is the system that we cannot afford—unless we raise taxes *and* cut benefits substantially. By 2040, the Social Security trustees project a cost rate (the payroll tax) of 26.97 percent of wages to finance Social Security and Medicare Part A (HI).

In this state of affairs, everyone involved will feel cheated. Young workers will feel that they are shouldering an unfair burden of extra taxes. The older generation will suffer, because their promised benefits will be cut. America's economic well-being will be diminished, because more and more private income will be taxed and taken out of the private sector where it is needed for investment in economic growth and job creation.

Under the Tier 2 system I have proposed, the future of Social Security is redeemed, and can be financed by putting the higher rates of return—normally realized in the private sector—to work for us. Under the system we have now, there is no financial help from investment in the private sector. Under the Tier 2 funded system, workers will be able to tap into the power of compound interest, and their money will grow an estimated 8 percent per year over a forty-five to fifty-year period. The dynamic growth of the private sector will enable you to become a millionaire, and will allow America to afford an aging population.

THE CHOICE: PAY-AS-YOU-GO VS. FUNDED SOCIAL SECURITY

Under the pay-as-you-go system, we can:

1. Raise taxes, and then raise taxes again.
2. Cut benefits, and then cut benefits again.
3. Create no new capital ownership opportunities.
4. Drain an increasing amount of America's resources—our savings and investment—out of the private sector. A shrinking private sector damages our ability to create new jobs and new industries—our future strength.
5. View the American economy as a shrinking pie, and sit back and watch the young generation and the older generation fight over the slices.

Under the proposed Tier 2 system, we can:

1. Cut payroll taxes by two percentage points once the transition years are completed.
2. Increase benefits as the system matures, and capital accumulates.
3. Create **100 million** millionaires.
4. Amass unprecedented savings and investment in America by opening the doors of capital ownership to all Americans and use our **$50 trillion** to **$100 trillion** capital pool to finance high-paying jobs and new industries for tomorrow.
5. Unleash new economic growth and create a new standard whereby all Americans will have income from wages and capital.

HERE'S HOW—STEP BY STEP

Step 1: Keep Our Existing Promises
Keep our existing promises to individuals who are currently retired and who are receiving Social Security benefits. They paid their money into Social Security and will retain the Social Security benefits as promised under the existing system.

More affluent retirees, who are not dependent on Social Security for a comfortable lifestyle in retirement, will also retain their benefits. As described in Step 7, they will have the opportunity to purchase Liberty Bonds, which will transfer their benefits, with interest, to their heirs—tax-free.

**Step 2:
Create Tier 2
Capital
Set-asides**

Create the $500 to $3,000 per year set-asides into personal investment and retirement accounts established with one of the management firms approved by the Grow America Corporation.

For a detailed description of the set-aside system, please see the section "Individual Participation" in Chapter 7, "Save Social Security". An analysis of the 1994 *Statistical Supplement* shows that the criteria for individual participation qualify 100 million Americans— 80 percent of the work force. Begin the large-scale Tier 2 set-asides into the individual investment accounts in 1996 at $111.5 billion and increase to $152.0 billion in 2015, $169.1 billion in 2025, $223.0 billion in

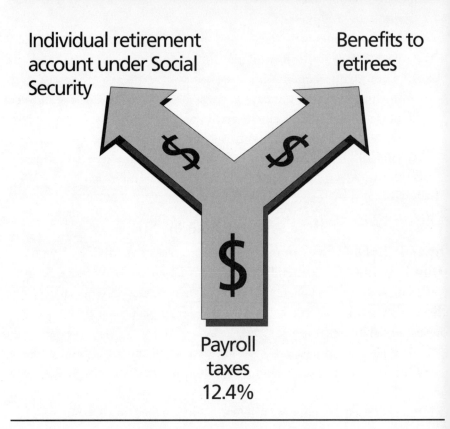

New Social Security: A Two-Tier System

Individual retirement account under Social Security

Benefits to retirees

Payroll
taxes
12.4%

2050, and $273.0 billion by 2070. These investment set-asides will utilize hundreds of billions of dollars that otherwise would pay Social Security benefits. How can we afford the set-asides in the transition years?

Step 3: Use Existing Surpluses to Fund Individual Retirement Accounts

From 1996 through 2012 Social Security projects annual surpluses in the range of $25 billion per year. Stop using these monies to pay other government bills, and start funding our individual accounts. We're being taxed for *retirement*. Let's use the money that way.

Step 4: Cap the Social Security Trust Fund and Pay the IOUs

At year end 1995, the government owed the Social Security Trust Fund $475.4 billion. At 6.3 percent regular interest, paying off this debt over the next twenty years will add $29.9 billion a year to the individual funded accounts from 1996 through 2015.

Step 5: Start Using Income from the Tier 2 Accounts to Pay Social Security Benefits and Reduce the Tier 1 Tax Burden

Even though the amount is very small, income from the Tier 2 capital accounts begins at the end of Year 1. At that time, the first group of participants, who have accumulated capital in their personal investment and retirement accounts for one year, are retiring. They begin to receive interest income to offset the Tier 1, pay-as-you-go tax burden. Income from capital in the system will be $19.9 billion in 2010, build to $169.2 billion in 2030, reach $496.2 billion in 2050, and rise to $576.9 billion in 2070.

Step 6: Retain Social Security Tier 1 as a Safety Net

The goal is to save Social Security. Current retirees will retain their benefits. Although the federal government cannot guarantee that all private sector investments will increase in value, the government will be able to guarantee Safety Net benefits under the Tier 1 system. A version of existing Social Security will remain to ensure a reasonable retirement income floor for all Americans.

Benefits from One Social Security Source

Payroll
taxes

To remodel Social Security for the twenty-first century, we can leave early retirement at sixty-two or sixty-five but raise the NRA to seventy over a thirty-four-year period. This adjustment can be completed in 2029. During the transition, we can raise indexing for real wage growth at half of 1 percent instead of 1 percent.

Step 7: Market Liberty Bonds To finance the existing pay-as-you-go system, the 1994–1995 Advisory Council discussions include many options to raise taxes. One short-term Advisory Council option increases taxes 2.3 percent in 1998, which keeps the system solvent until 2021. Then taxes will have to be raised again. An alternative long-term option raises taxes 4.9 percent in 1998. Under this approach we don't have to raise taxes again until 2056.

Benefits from Two Social Security Sources

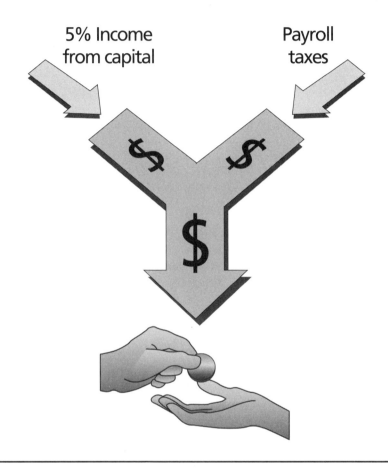

5% Income
from capital

Payroll
taxes

I considered including in my proposal a plan to raise taxes 2 percent starting in 1996 to finance the two-tier system, but discarded it. I am committed to no new taxes. If implemented, a 2 percent tax increase would raise, at twenty-year intervals, $57.8 billion in 1996, $79.4 billion in 2016, and $97.8 billion in 2036. So a 2 percent tax increase would balance the two-tier system. But I prefer an alternative approach. My assumption is that Americans are truly fed up with tax increases.

Instead of raising taxes, I propose to create a new financial instrument— Liberty Bonds. Liberty Bonds will appeal to Americans' sense of fairness and pride. Offer Americans the opportunity to trade promised Social

Security benefits which come due from 1996 through 2025—a thirty-year period—for a future benefit. They have paid money throughout their working lives into Social Security, and they reasonably expect benefits. They expect to receive $7,500, $10,000, or $15,000 per year until their death and the death of their spouse for an average of eighteen years—based on current life expectancy.

For most, Social Security is essential to support retirement. Others, with more adequate retirement income, can opt to defer Social Security payments. Liberty Bonds will provide a voluntary way to defer receipt of Social Security money, and pass the value of this money on after thirty years—2026–2055—to your heirs or other individuals of your choice. Using the tax code, we can make the trade-off financially attractive. By deferring income now, allow Americans the choice of helping the next generation with education, home ownership, new business opportunities, or medical trust funds.

Millions of individuals will set aside $1,000 per year after retirement for their remaining lifetimes to create a $25,000 nest egg for their heirs. Others will choose to set aside $2,000 per year to create a $50,000 tax-free education fund for their grandchildren. Many will agree to set aside their full Social Security benefit—$10,000 to $15,000 per year for their lifetimes.

The savings from the purchase of Liberty Bonds are projected at $60 billion in 1996, $70 billion in 1999, $75 billion in 2002, and more thereafter. The government can create a cap of $95 billion per year through 2025 on the amount of the allowed set-asides so that no more money is deferred than is necessary. This rises and can be capped in 2014 at $95 billion per year through 2025.

The purpose of the Liberty Bonds is to prevent a tax increase and to defer promised government costs for thirty years while the two-tier system is being put in place.

The business world offers us an important analogy. If a business is on the verge of bankruptcy (costs are quadrupling, and income remains the same), one solution is to defer creditors by asking them to accept later payment. The business will bring in a large infusion of new capital, and pay off the creditors once profits return.

Similarly, Liberty Bonds will infuse capital into Social Security. I anticipate that five million to ten million Americans will agree to purchase

AFFORDING THE TRANSITION		
	Annual amount	Years
1. Use existing surpluses.	$25 billion	1–17
2. Pay off trust fund debt.	$30 billion	1–20
3. Market Liberty Bonds.	$60 billion–$95 billion	1–30
4. Use income from capital.	$20 billion–$589 billion	1–75

Liberty Bonds. This will save Social Security up to $60 to $95 billion per year during the thirty years from 1996 to 2025. If a voluntary plan does not work, rather than raise taxes, I recommend implementing the Liberty Bond system on a mandated basis. If necessary, a scaled formula could be created whereby Liberty Bonds—or their equivalent—would become mandatory.

HOW TO MODERNIZE THE PRIVATE PENSION SYSTEM

We need to recognize at the outset that there are no simple ways to adapt the private pension system to the modern workplace. Employers are faced with major competitive pressures as they join the world marketplace. Big business is looking to scale back and cut costs—especially pension and health care costs. And small business is always on the edge fighting for survival. Most employees are happy to have jobs, and are not in a position to create waves.

But employees will be living longer, and the quality of their lives after retirement is dependent on having decent pension income. Therefore, here are four broad recommendations which offer a suggested path to reform.

1. The Importance of Economic Education Employers and employees alike need to focus explicitly on the changing nature of the workplace. Increased life expectancy means that all of us need to plan carefully for retirement and that we need private pensions—funded, without interruption, throughout our working lifetimes—a forty-five- to fifty-year period. Employees need to learn about the value of saving, compound interest, investment alternatives, reasonable rates of return, and the importance of professional financial management. Education about money and its workings is essential before employees can begin to look out for themselves and become independent as operating citizens.

Special economic education curricula need to be developed and made available nationally in schools and at the local and state level. These efforts need to be broad in scale and sustained over many years. Employers should offer financial planning services to employees (many already do).

2. Fairness   Americans want to be fair. Through economic education two basic concepts need to become part of our common understanding. The first is the imperative of planning for economic security after retirement. The second (to be fully described in Chapter 14) is a new standard—creating capital as a second source of income for our children.

As these ideas gain common acceptance, the availability of private pensions, immediate vesting, and portability will follow in practice. Employers almost always take care of their own personal retirement and will realize the imperative nature of these decisions for all employees.

3. The Trend toward Defined Contribution 401(k) Pensions   As the trend toward defined contribution 401(k) pensions continues, individuals will become better educated about the value of money and savings, the need for professional management, and compound interest.

Under defined benefit plans, businesses and other employers have the responsibility of setting money aside and investing the money so that employees receive promised benefits.

Under 401(k)s however, employees own the assets and receive frequent statements showing the capital growth. Employees take a direct interest, and as shareholders, are learning about money.

4. Special Small Business Initiatives   In the private sector, the major pension gap occurs in the small business sector. Many small business owners are not familiar with their options and many—especially start-ups—do not have the liquidity and resources to fund pensions.

A carefully designed national marketing effort, tailored to small business, can have an important economic impact. The marketing plan needs to focus on three basic issues:

- How the employers/owners best benefit personally. This remains the most powerful entry point.
- How employers can establish a pension system—cost free to the business—and offer the benefits—on a voluntary basis—to all employees.
- Establishing TIAA-CREF models specifically for small business on either a matching employer-employee basis or an employee-only voluntary basis.

Shareholders in a Stronger America

On a combined basis, funding Social Security Tier 2 individual accounts and stressing savings through private pensions will involve over 100 million Americans as shareholders in our economic future. Personal participation will make savings and economic education part of everyone's day-to-day life experience. Just as individuals who own their homes know everything about their mortgages and the fair market value of their property, so individuals who own capital will become quite knowledgeable about their portfolios and capital accumulation. The benefits of this knowledge for individuals and families will include increased economic capability, a confident sense of the future, and more power to make the fundamental choices that affect their lives.

12

Social Security: Honoring the Contract

In 1929, when America faced its most devastating economic crisis, one possible response was for private business and government to yield to despair—to retrench and cut back on everything. President Franklin Roosevelt took the opposite approach. In the face of adversity, the president's message was one of growth, creativity, and hope. Under FDR's leadership, Social Security was enacted in the midst of the Great Depression, and it has been endorsed and expanded by every succeeding president.

When the Social Security system was established, it was based on specific underlying principles. It is important to compare the proposed funded system with these principles. Over the sixty years of its existence, Social Security has come to be accepted as a sacred contract. The number every American knows is his or her own Social Security number. The goal of my plan is to save Social Security, not destroy it.

Three major national organizations serve as watchdogs to protect the rights of senior citizens—the American Association of Retired Persons (AARP), the National Committee to Preserve Social Security and Medicare, and the National Council of Senior Citizens.

AARP representatives, in their March 1995 testimony before the 1994–1995 Advisory Council, eloquently outlined the founding principles of Social Security:

- Benefits are an earned right.
- Benefits are related to pay and time in the work force.
- Benefits are not based on need but are provided on a progressive basis.

As individuals work throughout their lives, they pay money they have earned into Social Security. Individuals who work more years receive larger benefits. Individuals who have larger salaries pay more into Social Security and receive larger benefits. Social Security is not a welfare program based on the need of individuals after retirement, but is considered to be an earned right.

And this basic principle is strongly emphasized in the proposed Tier 2 funded Social Security system. The AARP testimony continues:

> In order to provide adequacy, however, the formula is weighted so lower-wage workers receive a benefit which replaces a higher percentage of their pre-retirement wages than it does for average and high earners. Weighting the benefit formula to favor lower-wage workers assures all workers and their families a floor of protection against poverty when a worker retires, becomes disabled or dies.

The existing progressive Social Security formula is reinforced in the proposed Tier 2 funded system. In fact, my proposal carries the idea even further. Under the proposed Tier 2 system, as we know, individuals earning $4,032 per year will set aside $500 per year into their funded accounts. Once the system reaches maturity—after forty-five years—they will have a $413,921 capital nest egg to pass on, if they wish, to their heirs tax-free. That's worth $73,697 in today's money. Their expected Social Security benefits under the old system, assuming no tax increase, will be $3,866 per year. At 5 percent income from capital, their benefits under my proposal will be $3,685, very close to the pay-as-you-go benefits—and they will still have the $73,697 to pass on to their heirs. If they choose an annuity, their annual income will be $5,822.

Individuals earning $8,000 per year will pay $992 per year into their personal accounts. After forty-five years, they will have accumulated $821,219—$146,215 in today's money. At 5 percent of income from capital, their benefits under the proposed plan will be $7,311 per year—*more* than they would get from the pay-as-you-go system—and, again, they can pass the $146,215 on tax-free to their heirs. By choosing an annuity, they will receive $11,550 per year—almost double regular Social Security. These are impressive increases from any standpoint, but the true excitement comes from the opportunity for all Americans to become substantial capital owners.

The AARP testimony continues, listing three additional principles which have become part of the Social Security system over the years. They are:

- The system is self-financed.
- Employees and employer contribute equally.
- Participation is compulsory.

These three important principles also remain in the proposed Tier 2 funded system. The personal accounts will be administered by private sector financial managers, but all Social Security payments will still be made to Social Security. The set-asides will go into individual named accounts with firms certified and regulated by the independent Grow America Corporation.

Participation remains compulsory. What is exciting is that in this way Social Security becomes a mandated savings system for all U.S. workers, making them shareholders in a stronger America. Just when our savings levels are becoming dangerously low, the proposed system will be adding $100 billion to $200 billion per year into savings and investment.

We have seen that the proposal is to set aside *existing* tax monies into a mandated savings plan, with no new taxes, and that the plan builds professional management into the operation. The system will have clear rules. The Tier 2 monies will be privately administered under Grow America regulation, and for a sole purpose—income and security for retirement and disability.

A COMMITMENT TO FINANCIAL INDEPENDENCE

The analysis in this book focuses on the difficult transition period and demonstrates that we can afford to continue our promises under the Tier 1, pay-as-you-go system and at the same time, set aside $100 billion to $200 billion per year into savings and personal investment accounts.

The analysis ends after seventy-five years in the year 2070. The seventy-fifth year shows a $303.9 billion annual surplus. The system will continue to show substantial surpluses. These surpluses can be used to cut payroll taxes and increase the annual set-asides as appropriate. Set-asides from existing tax dollars could increase to $6,000 per year on a sliding scale and could offer participants even greater capital accumulation.

BENEFITS FOR ALL

The various benefit levels in Social Security are complex. There are beneficiaries with and without spouses. There are individuals with dependents and individuals without dependents. There are disabled individuals with and without dependents. And many more variables. For each category of beneficiary there are different calculations and benefit levels. There is a direct correlation between the great variety of recipients and the system's diversity and its complexity.

◆

The goal of my proposal is to increase economic opportunity for all Americans, individually and as a nation. The major point is that investing $100 billion to $200 billion per year in savings and the private sector will provide a larger pool of resources to draw upon, and will place less strain on existing tax income.

◆

The proposal offers a vision of an expanding American economy and offers specific steps to achieve it.

◆

With more resources, the Social Security Administration will be in a better position to adjust its benefit formulas to best meet everyone's rights and needs. With more money, Social Security can better address the needs of nonworking spouses, part-time workers, divorcees, and elderly widows—who face the greatest hardships in the current system. By 2050, the Tier 2 system will be generating sufficient income to accommodate these adjustments as appropriate.

Once the system is funded across America, there are many bright options. To address them now is speculative and unnecessary. But I am confident that a fully funded operating system will afford all participants and policy makers exciting and positive choices.

FINANCING AMERICA'S THIRD CENTURY

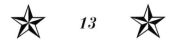

13

New Savings: Fuel to Run the American Economy

The brightness of your personal economic future and the country's economic future are directly connected, because individual savings and investments build the capital pools which create industries and jobs for tomorrow.

Before the start of America's first century of independence, Ben Franklin advised us on the importance of savings and on the promised miracle of compound interest. In *Advice to a Young Tradesman from an Old One,* he wrote:

> Remember that Money is of a prolific generating Nature. Money can beget money, and its offspring can beget more, and so on. Five Shillings Turn'd, is Six. Turn'd again 'tis Seven and Three Pence; and so on 'til it becomes an Hundred Pound. The more there is of it, the more it produces every Turning, so that Profits rise quicker and quicker.

When Franklin died in 1790, he left £1,000 pounds to Boston and £1,000 to Philadelphia (about $4,500 in today's money to each). The money was to be spent to help young tradesmen start their own businesses. In his will, Franklin left very specific terms controlling the money and its use. The money was to be invested and reinvested for the first 100 years to allow savings and compound interest to grow. Franklin estimated that each £1,000 would grow to £130,000—from $4,500 to $582,000 in 1892 money. By 1891, each city had $391,000.

After 100 years, three quarters of the money was to be spent on productive projects. Philadelphia created the Franklin Institute—the world-famous science museum. Boston created the Franklin Institute of Boston—a technical college awarding degrees in engineering and industrial chemistry, which still operates today.

The remaining quarter of the money was to be loaned for the next 100 years to help start businesses and additional community projects. Thousands of individuals and projects were assisted, and after 200 years the remaining principal became part of the endowments of the two Franklin Institutes—$2.3 million in Philadelphia and $4.5 million in Boston.

In the early 1900s, Henry Pritchett, one of the Franklin fund managers and president of the Massachusetts Institute of Technology (MIT), met with Andrew Carnegie, who was impressed with the idea of putting the power of compound interest to work to help build retirement nest eggs for America's teachers. In this way, Franklin's concept became part of the birth of the TIAA-CREF system described earlier. Ben Franklin's concept mirrors exactly the point of this book.

There are eighty years left in America's third century of independence. Let's make them count! With Tier 2 funded Social Security, each worker will have a personal investment and retirement account and will be in a position to heed Ben Franklin's advice and reap the rewards. Every worker earning $10,000 or more can become a millionaire in one working lifetime. As a nation, we will be setting $100 billion to $200 billion aside each year into these accounts.

By 2010, the accumulated capital owned by retirees and their heirs will be an estimated $384 billion—by 2030, $3.9 trillion; by 2050, an estimated $14.6 trillion; and by 2070 an estimated $27.3 trillion. By 2076, we will be well into the second working lifetime under funded Social Security.

If we increase financial opportunity for all Americans, no nation can compete with America's ability to amass capital. These pools of capital

ACCUMULATED CAPITAL OWNED BY RETIREES AND THEIR HEIRS

By 2010	$384 billion
By 2030	$3.9 trillion
By 2050	$14.6 trillion
By 2070	$27.3 trillion

are the source of investment which can be directed to finance thousands and thousands of industries in America and around the world. These new industries will create jobs and purchasing power and economic growth.

The promise of increased savings is welcome at a time when America's savings are dangerously shrinking. Please see the figure "Net Private Savings."

Between 1960 and today, national private savings available for investment in industry and jobs have dropped from 8.1 percent of GDP to under 1.7 percent. This decline in investment capital is a major factor

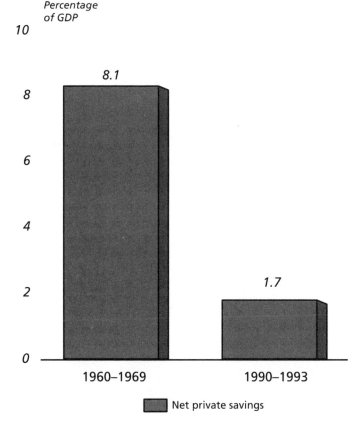

Net Private Savings

Percentage of GDP

Net private savings

Source: Bipartisan Commission on Entitlement and Tax Reform, Final Report to the President, *J. Robert Kerrey chairman, John C. Danforth vice-chairman (Washington, D.C.: U.S. Government Printing Office, January 12, 1995).*

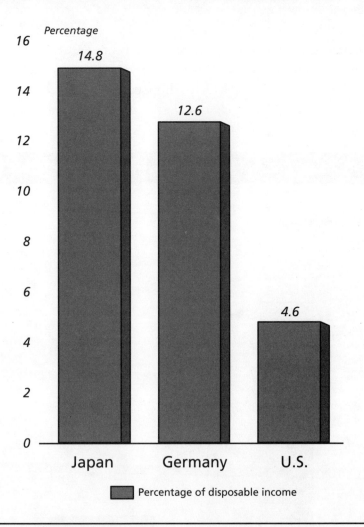

Savings Crisis

Source: *Merrill Lynch,* Individual Retirement Accounts: Saving the American Dream *(New York, 1995).*

leading to loss of jobs and job security. If we compare savings in America with savings in other nations, America lags far behind. In 1993, U.S. household savings as a percentage of disposable personal income was 4.6 percent, in contrast to 12.3 percent in Germany and 14.8 percent in Japan. Please see the figure "Savings Crisis." Funded Social Security could reverse this dangerous trend.

Social Security and pension experts in Washington raise the most important corresponding issue. If, as fast as we build individual savings, an overgrown government borrows those monies to pay its annual deficits and service the national debt, then there are no *net new* savings. There is no *new* capital for private sector investment and economic growth.

Let's review the impact of funding Social Security on net new savings from 1996 through 2025. The goal is to create a savings and endowment society. In the first thirty years of the new plan—1996–2025—the money being set aside into the individual investment and retirement accounts will come from four main sources:

1. Social Security Surpluses: $25 Billion per Year, 1996–2012

Over the next seventeen years, Americans will pay extra taxes for Social Security and retirement—creating surpluses averaging $25 billion per year, through 2007, and then dwindling to $.8 billion in 2012—the last estimated surplus year. These surpluses total $367.6 billion.

During these years $25 billion of the annual funding for individual Tier 2 accounts will come from these surpluses. The Congress must reduce federal spending by these amounts—and then a large percentage of this $25 billion a year will become net new savings.

2. Retiring the Existing Social Security Trust Fund Debt: $29.9 Billion per Year, 1996–2015

As you know from Chapter 11, the government has borrowed $475.4 billion from the trust fund to pay for other programs and debt. The proposed plan calls for paying off this debt at $29.9 billion per year over the next twenty years. This totals $598 billion. The Congress will have to reduce federal spending by an additional $29.9 billion, and then most of the $29.9 billion will become net new savings.

Inside the Washington beltway, most observers will scoff at the oversimplification of these assertions. They rightly will point to the handwringing and posturing by politicians seeking to balance the budget by the year 2000 or 2005. Politicians are in a very difficult crossfire. There is little doubt that a national debt spiraling out of control bodes ill for our future, but the politicians only reflect the demands their constituents are actually putting on them for more government spending.

Disillusioned Washington observers will point to our experience over the past twenty years. The nation has witnessed thousands and thousands of speeches on the importance of balancing the budget, matched with the doubling, tripling, and quadrupling of the national debt. The national debt was $533 billion in 1975 and has grown almost tenfold to over $5 trillion as we head into 1996.

This book contains three major messages.

- The first is one of great individual hope: We can create true economic opportunity for all. Financial independence is within our reach.
- Government spending for entitlements threatens the very safety of America's future—unless we develop bold new approaches.
- The way out is to build our institutions around a savings, investment, and endowment society, producing benefits for older Americans and opportunity for younger Americans.

The true problems of government spending will not be realized until roughly 2020–2030, when the baby boomers will have retired en masse. Handwringing in 1996 about how to balance the budget by 2000 or 2005 has no comparison with the scale of problems just around the corner.

In 2020, Social Security will show a $100 billion annual deficit; Medicare Part A (HI), a $200 billion annual deficit; and Medicare Part B (SMI), an additional $200 billion deficit—totaling $500 billion as an annual deficit. By 2040, this builds to a $1 trillion annual deficit.

The American experience is built on individual dreams, on being practical, and on being prepared to sacrifice and take risks. In this context, a leadership appeal to sacrifice to save America and to create a bright future for our children can build the necessary national support to cut spending by $50 billion to $55 billion per year—now.

Leaders willing to engage this issue—on a nonpartisan and united basis—need to talk directly to the American people. Let these leaders say, "Cutting government spending is difficult, but essential. All of us are worried about America's future. We need to create a savings and investment society. All the proceeds from these cuts will go directly into your personal investment and retirement accounts. Let's join together to fulfill the promises of the Founding Fathers."

Individual citizens will respond to the need to rally America—especially if the necessary cuts flow dollar for dollar into their individual savings accounts. Cuts of $50 to $55 billion per year today are more manageable than cuts of $500 billion per year twenty-five years from now.

3. LIBERTY BONDS: $60 BILLION TO $95 BILLION PER YEAR, 1996–2025

The sale of Liberty Bonds will cut government spending on Social Security by $60 billion to $95 billion per year from 1996–2025. Individual Americans will be forgoing current Social Security benefits, deferring them, tax-free, with interest, to their children and heirs. After thirty years, the capital in the individual accounts will have built up, and the extra income generated by the private sector will help to pay off the Liberty Bonds.

Calculating our net new savings based on Liberty Bonds is not easy. Assume that these monies would have been taxed—an estimated $26 per $100. Then assume that 50 percent of these monies would have been used by the recipients as savings or investment. The assumption is that individuals buying the Liberty Bonds can afford to defer this income, and that large amounts of this money would have ended up in savings. Net new savings then become $37 per $100. Every $100 billion of Liberty Bonds therefore creates $37 billion of net savings.

4. THE IMPACT OF VOLUNTARY SAVINGS MATCHES

Under the proposed plan many millions of participating workers will add a voluntary savings match to their annual Tier 2 set-asides. These savings matches can begin at $31.8 billion per year in 1996 and build to $48.2 billion per year by 2025. It is assumed that 50 percent of these monies will become net new savings. Please see the Net New Savings table, which summarizes estimated net new savings under the plan. Net new savings for 1996–2025 total $2.3 trillion—and average $76.7 billion per year.

Net new savings are the fuel that runs America's economic future. When we fund Social Security, our personal interests and the national interest become the same. Once the funded system reaches maturity, the great majority of these capital set-asides will *all* be net new savings. The impact on available capital investment pools and on economic growth will be enormous.

Net New Savings (in billions of dollars)

Year	Existing Social Security surpluses (80%)	Pay off trust fund $29.9 B/yr. (80%)	Liberty Bonds $37 per $100 (37%)	Savings matches (50%)	Total
1996	21.2	23.9	22.2	15.9	83.2
1997	21.2	23.9	22.2	16.2	83.5
1998	20.8	23.9	22.2	16.5	83.4
1999	20.7	23.9	25.9	16.9	87.4
2000	20.9	23.9	25.9	17.2	87.9
2001	20.6	23.9	25.9	17.5	87.9
2002	19.9	23.9	27.7	17.9	89.4
2003	19.6	23.9	27.7	18.2	89.4
2004	20.0	23.9	27.7	18.5	90.1
2005	20.3	23.9	29.6	18.8	92.6
2006	19.0	23.9	29.6	19.1	91.6
2007	17.6	23.9	29.6	19.4	90.5
2008	16.2	23.9	31.4	19.7	91.2
2009	14.9	23.9	31.4	20.0	90.2
2010	13.4	23.9	31.4	20.4	89.1
2011	07.0	23.9	33.3	20.6	84.8
2012	00.6	23.9	33.3	20.9	78.7
2013	00.0	23.9	33.3	21.1	78.3
2014	00.0	23.9	33.3	21.4	78.6
2015	00.0	23.9	33.3	21.7	78.9
2016	00.0	00.0	33.3	21.9	55.2
2017	00.0	00.0	33.3	22.2	55.5
2018	00.0	00.0	33.3	22.4	55.7
2019	00.0	00.0	33.3	22.7	56.0
2020	00.0	00.0	35.1	22.9	58.0
2021	00.0	00.0	35.1	23.2	58.3
2022	00.0	00.0	35.1	23.4	58.5
2023	00.0	00.0	35.1	23.6	58.7
2024	00.0	00.0	35.1	23.9	59.0
2025	00.0	00.0	35.1	24.1	59.2
Totals	294.1	478.0	921.3	608.2	2,301.6

14

Create a Second Source of Income for Yourself and Your Children

There are two main sources of income: First, through their labor, individuals receive payment—usually wages. Capital is the second source of income. That is, as we have seen, money makes money: capital earns dividends and interest, and equity grows.

The easiest way to understand labor and capital is briefly to look back in history. The earliest civilizations began as agrarian societies. People worked the fields. The result of their labor was food. Food meant survival and surpluses could be traded, or sold for money. In an agrarian society, the capital was land. Historically, ownership of land was concentrated in the hands of a few—kings and queens, the nobility, and (in the West) the church. An important motivation for many who came to America was to break the European lock on land ownership by the ecclesiastical and upper classes: In America everyone could own land.

Economic life was largely agrarian from the beginning of civilization until the mid-1800s when the industrial revolution became predominant. From 1850 to the present, the primary source of income to American families has remained income from wages. But, the new standard is for you and your children to have a second source of income.

AFFLUENCE IN AN INDUSTRIAL SOCIETY

Opening the benefits of capital ownership to all Americans is a breakthrough idea. In a democracy, we are all shareholders in the political system with the power to vote. With capital ownership, we can all be shareholders in economic independence.

In the next forty-five to fifty years—one working lifetime—we have the opportunity as a nation to create 100 million capital owners with substantial equity assets in the range of $100,000 to $1 million and more. To make the idea of capital as a second source of income come alive, imagine that you win the lottery and receive a check for $100,000, $250,000, $500,000, or $1 million. Overnight, you have become a capital owner. Having a capital base—having principal—creates an income stream for you.

- A capital base of **$100,000** can provide **$6,000** to **$8,000** of income per year.
- A capital base of **$250,000** can provide **$15,000** to **$20,000** of income per year.
- A capital base of **$500,000** can provide **$30,000** to **$40,000** of income per year.
- A capital base of **$1,000,000** can provide **$60,000** to **$80,000** of income per year.

Through a funded Social Security system and through pensions, you can accumulate capital. Simple reports will tell you:

- This is the value of your capital.
- This is the amount of money set aside this year for you in your account.
- As a capital owner, this is the amount of money you made this year through interest, dividends, and capital growth.

Few of us win the lottery, but through the pension system and the proposed changes in Social Security, each of us can gain a second income—and 100 million of us can become millionaires.

The late Louis Kelso, a San Francisco attorney, was a strong advocate of democratic capital ownership for over forty years. Along with Senator Russell Long of Louisiana, Kelso was the father of Employee Stock Ownership Plans (ESOPs). Kelso's plan was to use government guarantees to allow all Americans the opportunity to build a $25,000 to $50,000 capital nest egg. His goal was to supplement wages with $2,500 to $5,000 of income from capital. Kelso's statements are simple and powerful: "The bulk of wealth is produced, not by human labor as under preindustrial conditions, but by capital instruments. . . . Capital and not labor is the source of affluence in an industrial society."

Once capital is seen as the second source of income, the challenge becomes to find a mechanism to allow all Americans to have the opportunity to participate. Reforming Social Security and the pension system clearly offers each of us that opportunity. Meeting this challenge will create a capital revolution. The revolution is not an armed confrontation. The goal is not to take from the rich. The goal is to *become* rich. This is within the grasp of all of us.

If we achieve this, the capital revolution has every likelihood of stimulating a major period of economic growth. Imagine 50 million to 100 million Americans with an extra $10,000, $20,000, or $50,000 to spend each year. If we can combine income from labor and wages with new income from capital, the increased spending power can have a tremendous impact on economic growth.

THE FIRST ECONOMIC REVOLUTION: THE DEMOCRATIZATION OF WAGES

To continue our brief economic history, by the early 1900s the industrial revolution was full-blown. Large companies were emerging. Major new industries in textiles, steel, railroads, utilities, automobiles, and consumer products were everywhere. Cities were growing. Millions of immigrants were pouring into America, and they were mostly living in major metropolitan areas. The agrarian days of Thomas Jefferson's small farmer and rural society had passed.

The auto industry served as the most visible symbol of the industrial revolution and the age. Individual companies were employing thousands of workers. In 1910 General Motors employed 10,000; Studebaker employed 5,700; Packard, 4,640; and Ford, 2,595. By 1913 the Model T Ford was a huge success and Ford's labor force rose to 13,198.

Working and living conditions were crude by late-twentieth-century standards. Wages were low and hours were long. In 1908 production workers at Ford averaged $1.89 for a ten-hour day; by 1910 production men averaged $2.51 a day.

Henry Ford and the $5-a-Day Wage
In 1914 Henry Ford shook the industrial world when he announced a $5-a-day wage. Along with mass production, by offering workers a decent wage, Ford created the first economic revolution. As mass production and higher incomes spread to other segments

of the nation's industry, all Americans could afford consumer products. Workers could purchase cars, appliances, clothes, and housewares. This widespread new demand for these products stimulated industrial growth, created new jobs, and generated important economic multipliers. With the democratization of the first source of income—wages—the entire economy grew by leaps and bounds.

There are many stories, but no clear historical record, detailing the exact circumstances or motivations which led Ford to establish the $5-a-day wage, which has been called the "announcement that shook the country".

One explanation was that Ford Motor was realizing unprecedented profits, and Ford felt that workers deserved to share in the new wealth. In addition, the auto companies were faced with high turnover rates. Employees came and went; training new employees was expensive, and turnover hurt production. A $5-a-day wage could reduce turnover, help build corporate loyalty, and increase productivity.

Another variation of the story says that Ford was touring a plant with his son Edsel when two workers suddenly began to fight. Ford was upset that they had fought in front of Edsel, and began probing why they were battling. When Ford found that the fight had erupted because the men were under tremendous financial pressures because of their low wages, he decided to pay his workers more.

Yet another version is that Ford was running a directors' meeting, using a blackboard to figure out the proper wage level. He started at a $3 wage, then went up to $3.50, $4, and then $4.50. As the story goes, one board member was horrified. Sarcastically, he asked, "Why not $5?" "Why not?" Ford said, and made his decision. In any case, on January 5, 1914, the Ford directors unanimously approved the $5-a-day wage, reduced the work shift to eight hours, and created three shifts instead of two.

Alan Nevins in his biography *Ford: The Times, The Man, The Company,* describes the impact: "Ford's announcement was like the dazzling burst of a rocket in velvet skies. Headlines blazed throughout the globe." In a single stroke, Ford doubled existing wages and shocked the industrial world.

Most important, the $5-a-day wage became a symbol of the democratization of wages. And, while it was not the single cause of our unprecedented economic boom between 1910 and 1950, the $5-a-day wage remains one of the most famous turning points of American prosperity. Why was it so important?

The first economic revolution was stimulated by mass production and by providing workers with a decent wage. As their income increased, workers could buy more consumer goods. This increased the demand for new production, new factories, and new jobs. There is a direct connection between wages, demand, consumption, and production. In the 1920's, these increased wages allowed the average American to buy a car, clothes, appliances, and the full range of consumer goods. By opening the doors of opportunity, and by giving 50 million Americans ample spending power, the revolution of wages and labor was well underway. GNP statistics were not collected prior to 1929, but GNP reached $288.5 billion by 1950, and America was recognized worldwide as the preeminent economic power.

The Old Way: Wages Only

Economic Treadmill

You're working hard, and you're not getting anywhere. You have one source of income—wages only.

The New Way: Two Sources of Income and 100 Million Millionaires

Financial Independence

With a second income from capital, you can retire in comfort and save
your children's standard of living by passing the capital on tax-free.

THE SECOND ECONOMIC REVOLUTION:
THE DEMOCRATIZATION OF CAPITAL OWNERSHIP

If we combine the income from labor with the income from capital and
create 100 million millionaires, instead of being concerned about our
economic future, we will unleash a new economic growth matched only
by that in the period from 1910 to 1950.

The democratization of capital ownership can create the second
economic revolution in America. Imagine the increased spending power
and its impact. By the year 2050, there will be 74.26 million Americans
sixty-five and over—more than 20 percent of the population. Through
their pensions:

- If each has an extra **$10,000** of income from capital, this adds **$788.8 billion** to spending power every year.
- If each has an extra **$25,000** of income from capital, this adds **$1.972 trillion** to spending power every year.

A hundred million millionaires—It's not just a catchy number. What does it mean in terms of capital accumulation? If we multiply $1 million times 100 million individuals, we see that this equals $100 trillion of capital.

Current pension capital totals $4.2 trillion, and the accumulation is just beginning. In twenty-five years, this can become $25 trillion. We're already on that track. In fifty years, this can become $50 trillion as more people participate, and the capital grows further.

If you look at this progression, $100 trillion in less than one hundred years is within reach. The scale of these capital pools is mind-boggling: $25 trillion, $50 trillion, $100 trillion. All experts agree that capital investment leads to new industries, new job creation, and economic growth. These immense pools of capital will be truly revolutionary. Their potential to stimulate economic growth will be unprecedented.

Many people will point out the difficulty of finding sound investment opportunities for $100 trillion. But in 1910, anyone who predicted that Americans would own over 143 million cars in the early 1990s would have been considered wildly fanciful.

Once we've accumulated the capital, imagine the spending power our children can inherit. They will be the major beneficiaries of the second economic revolution. Instead of being the first generation in America to have a lower standard of living than their parents, our children will have opportunities few Americans can now dream of. The accumulation of capital, and the ability to pass it on to our children, can keep the American dream on track.

CAPITAL: A SECOND SOURCE OF INCOME

By the year 2070—only seventy-five years from now—50 million of our children could have a second income from capital.

- If each has an extra **$10,000** of income from capital, this adds **$500 billion** to spending power—every year.
- If each has an extra **$25,000** of income from capital, this adds **$1.25 trillion** to spending power—every year.

- If each has an extra **$50,000** of income from capital, this adds **$2.5 trillion** to spending power—every year.

The second economic revolution has the potential to be as powerful as the first. The democratization of capital ownership and expanding income from a second source—capital—can have a similar impact. Think about it. Make sure you and your family participate.

SOCIAL SECURITY AND PENSION CAPITAL: A LEGACY TO SAVE OUR CHILDREN'S STANDARD OF LIVING

One of the strongest motivations in the American dream is, through hard work, to pass a better opportunity on to our children. Millions of Americans have sacrificed and endured every imaginable hardship to improve their children's lot. As Louis Armstrong sang in "Hello Brother," "A man. . . wants a chance to give his kids a better life. Well hello, brother, hello."

Presidential candidates in the 1980s and 1990s have addressed the future, and each has championed saving the American dream. One of the discouraging aspects of the past ten years in America is the growing fear that our children will be less well off in the future. Three major economic indicators make this fear a distinct possibility:

- Real wages in the decade of the 1980s rose an average of less than 1 percent.
- America is losing manufacturing jobs, and they are being replaced by service jobs. Manufacturing jobs are high-paying; most service jobs are lower-paying. A server at a fast food restaurant earns substantially less than half the wages of an auto worker or a steel worker.
- As the American economy becomes part of the new world economy, many of our American high-paying jobs are moving to countries that pay lower wages.

Capital accumulation offers all of us an opportunity to reverse this picture. If we change our inheritance laws and allow Social Security and pension capital to be passed on tax-free to our children, we will create a second income for them—income from capital. Under the reforms proposed in this book, this is a very possible dream. If inflation is kept in reasonable check, individuals can live comfortably on the income from their investment and retirement accounts. Then they can pass the capital base on to their children.

Any tax proposal requires close federal scrutiny. Current federal expenditures seriously outstrip federal revenues. We need a balanced budget, and we shouldn't continue adding to the national debt. Although it is not within the purview of this book to undertake a long-term and detailed econometric revenue analysis, common sense and three specific factors strongly favor allowing Social Security and pension capital to be passed on to our children tax free.

First, the proposed tax-free inheritance of Social Security and pension assets does not represent the loss of any substantial existing federal revenue. There is no Social Security capital today to be taxed. Most pension assets are in defined benefit plans, and are not subject to inheritance tax. As a result, under this proposal, the federal government loses little existing revenue.

Second, the newly accumulated capital will become a major source of new tax revenue for the federal government in the future. All income derived from capital is taxable as ordinary income. Seniors receiving income from capital are taxed. Children inheriting the capital tax free will pay tax on the income they derive from it.

Third, a major objective of federal tax policy is to accumulate capital and savings in the national economy. There is broad acceptance that savings and capital accumulation are important to help America compete globally. Part of this federal tax policy objective is also to promote capital accumulation so that seniors will have economic security after retirement. The parable about killing the golden goose applies here. Once you painstakingly build the capital base over a fifty- to one-hundred-year period, it is counterproductive and short-sighted to double tax the capital foundation at death.

Our children can become the first generation to benefit from the capital revolution. All of us can dream again, and pass our dreams on, generation after generation.

IMPLICATIONS FOR INTERNATIONAL COMPETITIVENESS: AMERICA AS NUMBER ONE

These capital pools will offer America an important weapon in international economic competition. The scale of our pension assets was unimaginable forty-five years ago. American pension assets already exceed the GNP of both Japan and Germany, and the creation of a future $50 trillion to $100 trillion capital pool is unmatchable by any foreign competitor.

The strength of America depends on the strength of each individual. The two are inseparable in a democracy. If we launch a broad-scale campaign for capital ownership, build the excitement of becoming a millionaire, dramatize how capital ownership can save our children's standard of living—we can make individual Americans, our families, and our country economically stronger. We can translate the rhetoric about savings and investment into hard currency and assets. We can squander our position of leadership, or we can rise to the challenge of the global economy and build on it.

Currently no nation can compete with the ability of the United States to accumulate capital. The news media report that Japan and other foreign nations are buying America. Foreign investors now own Rockefeller Center, over 25 percent of downtown Los Angeles, and the Seattle Mariners. But, as I have pointed out earlier, no nation has the economic strength to amass a $50 trillion to $100 trillion capital base over the brief period of one working lifetime.

As we head into the twenty-first century, capital accumulation will be a determining factor in world leadership. America begins with a distinct advantage. By designing systems to open ownership opportunities on a democratic basis, we can create new levels of wealth. If we deliver the promise of capitalism to all our citizens, we can help ensure a third century of preeminence for America.

★ *15* ★

Take Action for Change

To save Social Security and to change the pension system to meet the needs of the modern workplace—to make it possible for 100 million Americans to become millionaires—we need to join together and take action for change. Speaking our minds and taking charge of our future is part of the fundamental promise of America.

Everything proposed in this book can be achieved. You just need to do two simple things:

- Sign up! Check the statements on the Shareholder's form and send them to me with your name and address via E-mail—or use a stamp.
- Tell others about the plan.

The need to get reforms underway is urgent. There is only a five- to eight-year window within which we can afford to change the Social Security system and create the personal investment and retirement accounts I describe. If we wait until 2020 or 2030, the baby boomers will have retired in large numbers, and the nation will no longer be able to afford the set-asides into individual accounts. The best opportunity will come right after the 1996 presidential election, in the first six months of 1997.

Together, we can become a mighty force for change. But we need to act now.

169

Count Me In as a Shareholder in America's Future

____ Yes! I want to be a shareholder in America's future. Let's make America grow!

____ Yes! I like the idea of having my own personal investment and retirement account under Social Security.

____ This will restore my faith in Social Security, because I will know the money is there, in my personal account.

____ Yes! I understand that Sam Beard proposes a two-tier system to save Social Security. I want to support the proposal and join in a citizens' effort.

____ Yes! I favor immediate vesting and portability in the pension system.

____ Yes! I know that having two sources of income—one from labor and wages and the other from capital—is important to provide retirement income for me and to save the standard of living of all our children. I want to be able to pass my money tax-free on to my heirs after my death and the death of my spouse.

____ Yes! Please add my name to your E-mail list.

____ Yes! I want to tell others about the proposed reforms. Please send me the talking points.

Count me in!
via E-mail at **sbeard@econ.org**
by mail at Sam Beard, Save Social Security, 621 Delaware Street, New Castle, DE 19720.

Please print name _____

Address _____

City, State, Zip _____

Telephone Number _____

E-mail Address _____

CHAPTER SOURCES

APPENDIX

BIBLIOGRAPHY

Chapter Sources

Chapter 1, "Time for a Declaration of Financial Independence"

James MacGregor Burns, *A People's Charter: The Pursuit of Rights in America* (New York: Alfred A. Knopf, 1991), 40–41.

Declaration of Independence, in *A History of the American People,* vol 1, ed. Harry J. Carman, Harold C. Syrett, and Bernard W. Wishy (New York: Alfred A. Knopf, 1960) appendix 1, 759.

Clinton Rossiter, *Seedtime of the Republic* (New York: Harcourt, Brace, 1953) 63–65.

Chapter 2, "Life, Liberty, and Property"

Jennifer Dixon, "Poll Finds Young Americans Doubt Social Security Future," *Washington Post,* Tuesday, September 27, 1994, sec. C.

Arthur B. Kennickell and Louise R. Woodburn, *Estimation of Household Net Worth Using Model-Based and Design-Based Weights: Evidence from the 1989 Survey of Consumer Finances* (Washington, D.C.: Federal Reserve Board, April, 1992), table 1.

Frank Luntz and Mark Siegel, *Social Security: The Credibility Gap,* Analysis of Third Millennium Survey (New York: Third Millennium, September, 1994).

Steven R. Maguire, "Employer and Occupational Tenure: 1991 Update," *Monthly Labor Review,* June 1993, 45.

U.S. Bureau of Labor Statistics, Supplement to the Current Population Survey (Washington, D.C.: U.S. Government Printing Office, January, 1991).

Chapter 3, "Twelve Secrets They Don't Want You to Know"

Bipartisan Commission on Entitlement and Tax Reform, *Final Report to the President,* J. Robert Kerrey chairman, John C. Danforth vice-chairman (Washington, D.C.: U.S. Government Printing Office, January 1995), 4, 79.

Committee on Ways and Means, U.S. House of Representatives, *1994 Green Book: Overview of Entitlement Programs* (Washington, D.C.: U.S. Government Printing Office, July 15, 1994), 92–93.

Economic Report of the President, transmitted to the Congress February 1995 (Washington, D.C.: U.S. Government Printing Office).

Federal Old-Age and Survivors Insurance and Disability Insurance Trust Funds (OASDI), Board of Trustees, *1994 Annual Report,* House Document 103-231 (Washington, D.C.: U.S. Government Printing Office, April 12, 1994), 168, 176, 178, 182.

Federal Supplementary Medical Insurance Trust Fund (SMI), Board of Trustees, *1994 Annual Report,* House Document 103-229 (Washington, D.C.: U.S. Government Printing Office, April 12, 1994).

Gary Robbins and Aldona Robbins, *Salvaging Social Security: The Incredible Shrinking Trust Fund, and What We Can Do about It,* IPI Policy Report no. 130 (Lewisville, Tex.: Institute for Policy Innovation, April 1995), 1.

Dallas L. Salisbury, "Testimony before the Advisory Council on Social Security," March 9, 1995 (unpublished paper, Washington, D.C.), 2.

Advisory Council on Social Security, "Financing Approaches for Social Security Designed for 1994 Trustees Intermediate Assumptions," Working Paper (Washington, D.C., February 7, 1995), 3, 8.

Chapter 4, "Americans on a Treadmill"

Bipartisan Commission on Entitlement and Tax Reform, *Final Report to the President,* J. Robert Kerrey chairman, John C. Danforth vice-chairman (Washington, D.C.: U.S. Government Printing Office, January 1995), 4.

Federal Supplementary Medical Insurance Trust Fund (SMI), Board of Trustees, *1994 Annual Report,* House Document 103-229 (Washington, D.C.: U.S. Government Printing Office, April 12, 1994).

U.S. Small Business Administration, Office of Advocacy, *The Facts about Small Business* (Washington, D.C.: U.S. Government Printing Office, April 1994), 1; *Handbook of Small Business Data,* 1994 ed. (Washington, D.C.: U.S. Government Printing Office, April 1994), 7.

Chapter 5, "The Promise of Capital Ownership"

Federal Old-Age and Survivors Insurance and Disability Insurance Trust Funds (OASDI), Board of Trustees, *1994 Annual Report,* House Document 103-231 (Washington, D.C.: U.S. Government Printing Office, April 12, 1994), 182.

Ibbotson Associates, "Stocks, Bonds, and Inflation," *1992 Yearbook: Market Results for 1926–1991* (Chicago, 1992).

Information Please Almanac, 47th ed. (Boston and New York: Houghton Mifflin, 1994), 828.

Social Security Administration, Office of Research and Statistics, *Annual Statistical Supplement, 1994, to the Social Security Bulletin,* SSA Publication no. 13-11700 (Washington, D.C.: U.S. Department of Health and Human Services, August 1994), 173, table 4.B7.

U.S. Small Business Administration, Office of Advocacy, *The Facts about Small Business* (Washington, D.C.: U.S. Government Printing Office, April 1994).

Profiles based on interviews by Sam Beard. Material used by permission of subjects.

Chapter 6, "Find Out Where You Stand"

Merton Bernstein, *The Future of Private Pensions* (London: Free Press of Glencove, Division of Macmillan, 1964), 4.

Committee on Ways and Means, U.S. House of Representatives, *1994 Green Book: Overview of Entitlement Programs* (Washington, D.C.: U.S. Government Printing Office, July 15, 1994), 854, 861.

Federal Old-Age and Survivors Insurance and Disability Insurance Trust Funds (OASDI), Board of Trustees, *1994 Annual Report,* House Document 103-231 (Washington, D.C.: U.S. Government Printing Office, April 12, 1994), 182.

Jill D. Foley, and Joseph S. Piacentini, *EBRI Databook on Employee Benefits,* 2d ed., Employee Benefit Research Institute Education and Research Fund (Washington, D.C., 1992), 459.

Dan M. McGill, *The Fundamentals of Private Pensions,* 5th ed., Pension Research Council, Wharton School of Business, University of Pennsylvania (Philadelphia, 1984), 3–4.

Tom Woodruff, telephone interview by Sam Beard, November 11, 1994.

Chapter 7, "Save Social Security"

Henry J. Aaron, Barry P. Bosworth, and Gary T. Burtless, *Can America Afford to Grow Old? Paying for Social Security* (Washington, D.C.: Brookings Institution, 1989), 24, 39, 79.

Advisory Council on Social Security, "Financing (Funding) Approaches for Social Security Designed for 1994 Trustees Intermediate Assumptions," Working Paper (Washington, D.C., February 7, 1995), 3, 8.

Richard V. Burkhauser and Dallas L. Salisbury, eds., *Pensions in a Changing Economy*, Employee Benefit Research Institute Education and Research Fund and the National Academy on Aging (Washington, D.C., 1993), 5, 19, 20, 22, 24.

Committee on Ways and Means, U.S. House of Representatives, *1994 Green Book: Overview of Entitlement Programs* (Washington, D.C.: U.S. Government Printing Office, July 15, 1994), 103.

Federal Old-Age and Survivors Insurance and Disability Insurance Trust Funds (OASDI), Board of Trustees, *1994 Annual Report*, House Document 103-231 (Washington, D.C.: U.S. Government Printing Office, April 12, 1994), 12, 20, 57–58, 156, 161, 168, 176–177, 182.

Ibbotson Associates, "Stocks, Bonds, and Inflation," *1992 Yearbook: Market Results for 1926–1991* (Chicago, 1992).

Social Security Administration, "Male Covered Worker Rates (per Hundred) and Female Covered Worker Rates (per Hundred)," memorandum to Sam Beard, data from PROJ2.12 (Baltimore, 1995), 33, 35.

Social Security Administration, Office of Research and Statistics, *Annual Statistical Supplement, 1994, to the Social Security Bulletin*, SSA Publication no. 13-11700 (Washington, D.C.: U.S. Department of Health and Human Services, August 1994), 160, 171.

Chapter 8, "Has This Ever Worked Before?"

Henry J. Aaron, Barry P. Bosworth, and Gary T. Burtless, *Can America Afford to Grow Old? Paying for Social Security* (Washington, D.C.: Brookings Institution, 1989), 24, 39, 79.

Paul H. Boeker, "Developing Strong Capital Markets: Contrasting Latin American and East Asian Experience" (Paper presented at the Second Hemisphere Conference on Social Security, Pension Reform, and Capital Markets Development; the Inter-American Development Bank and the Institute of the Americas, Washington, D.C., June, 1995), 20.

James Brooke, "Quiet Revolution in Latin Pensions," *New York Times*, September 10, 1994, Business, 1.

Central Provident Fund Board, *CPF Members' Handbook* (Singapore, April 1985), 1, 3–4.

Peter Drucker, *The Unseen Revolution* (New York: Harper and Row, 1976).

Federal Old-Age and Survivors Insurance and Disability Insurance Trust Funds (OASDI), Board of Trustees, *1994 Annual Report*, House Document 103-231 (Washington, D.C.: U.S. Government Printing Office, April 12, 1994), 12, 20, 57–58, 156, 161, 168, 176–177, 182.

Federal Supplementary Medical Insurance Trust Fund (SMI), Board of Trustees, *1994 Annual Report*, House Document 103–229 (Washington, D.C.: U.S. Government Printing Office, April 12, 1994), 57–58.

John C. Goodman and Gerald L. Musgrave, *Patient Power: Solving America's Health Care Crisis* (Washington, D.C.: Cato Institute, 1992), 601–602, 603–604.

The International Center for Pension Reform (Santiago, Chile: ICPR, n.d.), 3, 9, 18.

Mark M. Klugman, *About the International Center for Pension Reform* (Santiago, Chile, 1995).

Rita Koselka, "A Better Way to Do It," *Forbes*, October 28, 1991, 158.

Matt Moffett, "Latin American Model for Financial Reform," *Wall Street Journal*, August 22, 1994, 1.

José Piñera, "The Chilean Experience" (Speech delivered at Cato Institute Public Policy Forum, Washington, D.C., April 28, 1995), 3, 8, 18.

Chapter 9, "Make the Private Pension System Fit the Modern Workplace"

Randy Barber and Jeremy Rifkin, *The North Will Rise Again: Pensions, Politics and Power in the 1980s* (Boston: Beacon Press, 1978), 22.

Bureau of the Census, *Current Population Survey: Income, Poverty and Valuation of Noncash Benefits,* Consumer Income Series (Washington, D.C.: U.S. Department of Commerce, March 1994), 60–188, table 1; *Historical Statistics of the United States: Colonial Times to 1970* (Washington, D.C.: U.S. Department of Commerce, 1975), 342.

Richard V. Burkhauser, and Dallas L. Salisbury, eds. *Pensions in a Changing Economy,* Employee Benefit Research Institute Education and Research Fund and the National Academy on Aging (Washington, D.C., 1993), 24–26.

Commerce News (U.S. Department of Commerce Washington, D.C.) September 29, 1994, table 2.

Congressional Research Service, *Joint Pension Trusteeship: An Analysis of the Visclosky Proposal* (Washington, D.C.: Library of Congress, February 20, 1990), 22.

Economic Report of the President, transmitted to the Congress February 1995 (Washington, D.C.: U.S. Government Printing Office), 274, table B-1.

Employee Benefit Research Institute, *Employment-based Retirement Income Benefits: Analysis of the 1993 Current Population Survey Supplement,* Employee Benefit Research Institute Education and Research Fund (Washington, D.C., 1994), 8–10.

Jill D. Foley and Joseph S. Piacentini, *EBRI Databook on Employee Benefits,* 2d ed., Employee Benefit Research Institute Education and Research Fund (Washington, D.C., 1992), 150–151.

Ibbotson Associates, "Stocks, Bonds, and Inflation," *1992 Yearbook: Market Results for 1926–1991* (Chicago, 1992).

Steven R. Maguire, "Employer and Occupational Tenure: 1991 Update, *Monthly Labor Review,* June 1993, 45.

Dallas L. Salisbury, interview by Sam Beard, December 6, 1994.

Teachers Insurance and Annuity Association, *TIAA Investment Supplement 1991* (New York, 1992), 14.

U.S. Bureau of Labor Statistics, *Supplement to the Current Population Survey* (Washington, D.C.: U.S. Government Printing Office, January 1991).

Chapter 10, "Let Your Money Make Money"

John Bogle, *Bogle on Mutual Funds* (New York: Richard D. Irwin, 1994), 3.

Chapter 11, "A Step-by-Step Plan"

Federal Old-Age and Survivors Insurance and Disability Insurance Trust Funds (OASDI), Board of Trustees, *1994 Annual Report,* House Document 103-231 (Washington, D.C.: U.S. Government Printing Office, April 12, 1994), 144, 156, 161,168, 176, 182.

Social Security Administration, Office of Research and Statistics, *Annual Statistical Supplement, 1994, to the Social Security Bulletin* (Washington, D.C.: U.S. Department of Health and Human Services, August 1994), 173, table 4.B7, 173.

Advisory Council on Social Security, "Financing Approaches for Social Security Designed for 1994 Trustees Intermediate Assumptions," Working Paper (Washington, D.C., February 7, 1995), 3, 8, 168, 176.

Chapter 12, "Social Security: Honoring the Contract"

Joseph Perkins, statement by the American Society of Retired Persons before the 1994–1995 Advisory Council on Social Security, Washington, D.C., March 8, 1995.

Chapter 13, "New Savings: Fuel to Run the American Economy"

Committee on Ways and Means, U.S. House of Representatives, *1994 Green Book: Overview of Entitlement Programs* (Washington, D.C.: U.S. Government Printing Office, July 15, 1994).

Economic Report of the President, transmitted to Congress February 1995 (Washington, D.C.: U.S. Government Printing Office).

Federal Old-Age and Survivors Insurance and Disability Insurance Trust Funds (OASDI), Board of Trustees, *1994 Annual Report,* House Document 103-231 (Washington, D.C.: U.S. Government Printing Office, April 12, 1994).

Federal Supplementary Medical Insurance Trust Fund (SMI), Board of Trustees, *1994 Annual Report,* House Document 103-229 (Washington, D.C.: U.S. Government Printing Office, April 12, 1994).

Benjamin Franklin, "Advice to a Young Tradesman from an Old One," in *Franklin's Way to Wealth, or, Poor Richard Improved* (New York: S. Wood, 1817).

Franklin Technical Institute, *The Codicil of the Will of Benjamin Franklin* (Boston, 1965).

Susan Grad, *Income of the Population Fifty-five or Older, 1992,* Social Security Administration, Office of Research and Statistics, SSA Publication no. 13-1187 (Washington, D.C.: U.S. Department of Health and Human Services, May 1994).

Information Please Almanac, 47th ed. (Boston and New York: Houghton Mifflin Company, 1994), 47, 69, 190, 211.

Institute for Research on the Economics of Taxation, *Pay-as-You-Go Entitlements, the Baby-Boom, and the Federal Budget: Facing Up To Reality,* IRET Policy Bulletin, no. 64 (Washington, D.C., November 7, 1994), 3.

Laurence J. Kotlikoff, *The U.S. Fiscal and Savings Crises: The Role of Entitlements* (Boston: Boston University, December 1994), 5.

Merrill Lynch, *Individual Retirement Accounts: Saving The American Dream* (New York 1995), 2.

Alan Siegel and Owen Andrews, eds., *Living Legacy: A History of the Franklin Institute of Boston and the Franklin Foundation* (Boston, 1993), 2, 5, 120.

Social Security Administration, Office of Research and Statistics, *Annual Statistical Supplement, 1994, to the Social Security Bulletin,* SSA Publication no. 13-1170 (Washington, D.C.: U.S. Department of Health and Human Services, August 1994).

Chapter 14, "Create a Second Source of Income for Yourself and Your Children"

Committee on Ways and Means, U.S. House of Representatives, *1994 Green Book: Overview of Entitlement Programs* (Washington, D.C.: U.S. Government Printing Office, July 15, 1994), 103.

Employee Benefit Research Institute, *Employment-based Retirement Income Benefits: Analysis of the 1993 Current Population Survey Supplement,* Employee Benefit Research Institute Education and Research Fund (Washington, D.C., 1994), 8.

Jill D. Foley and Joseph Piacentini, *EBRI Databook on Employee Benefits,* 2d ed., Employee Benefit Research Institute Education and Research Fund (Washington, D.C., 1992), 459.

"Hello Brother," Louis Armstrong, *What A Wonderful World* (Universal City, Calif.: MCA Records, Inc., 1988).

Information Please Almanac, 47th ed. (Boston and New York: Houghton Mifflin Company, 1994), 69, 190, 211.

Louis O. Kelso and Patricia Hetter, *Two-Factor Theory: The Economics of Reality* (New York: Vintage Books, 1967), 8.

National Income and Products Accounting of the United States, vol. 1, 1929–1958 (Washington, D.C. : U.S. Government Printing Office, 1994), 12.

Alan Nevins, *Ford: The Times, The Man, The Company* (New York: Charles Scribner's Sons, 1954), 523, 525, 527–528, 533–534.

Chapter 15, "Take Action for Change," is not annotated.

Appendix

Running the Numbers

In preparing my proposal, I have had the privilege of working with many of the nation's top financial experts who specialize in Social Security and Medicare. They include:

- Stephen C. Goss, deputy chief actuary, Office of the Actuary, U.S. Social Security Administration
- Stephen J. Entin, resident scholar, Institute for Research on the Economics of Taxation (IRET), formerly the deputy assistant secretary for economic policy at the U.S. Department of the Treasury, where he specialized in research on Social Security and the preparation of the annual reports of the board of trustees of the Social Security system
- Aldona Robbins, vice president of Fiscal Associates, Bradley Senior Fellow at the Institute for Policy Innovation, author of *The ABC's of Social Security*, formerly an economist in the Office of the Secretary at the U.S. Department of Labor, and senior economist in the Office of the Assistant Secretary for Economic Policy, U.S. Department of the Treasury, where she served the secretary as managing trustee of the Social Security and Medicare Trust Funds
- Gary Robbins, president of Fiscal Associates, formerly in the U.S. Department of the Treasury for sixteen years, holding positions including chief of the applied econometrics staff (1982–1985), assistant to the undersecretary for tax and economic affairs (1981–1982) and assistant to the director of the Office of Tax Analysis (1975–1981)
- Sylvester Schieber, director of the Research and Information Center at Watson Wyatt Worldwide, first research director at the Employee Benefit Research Institute (EBRI), and serving for over eight years at the U.S. Social Security Administration, ending as the deputy director, Office of Policy Analysis
- Bruce D. Schobel, corporate vice president and actuary, New York Life Insurance Company, former (1982–1983) staff actuary, National Commission on Social Security Reform, Executive Office of the President, and the senior adviser for policy, Office of the Commissioner, U.S. Social Security Administration (1987–1988)

I have spent at least 1,500 hours creating the numerical analyses which are the basis of this book. The experts I consulted were very generous of their time and guidance; they spent an additional 1,500 hours analyzing and reviewing these numbers. This equals a working year and a half of combined effort.

The numbers are all based on official government reports. In each section of this Appendix, please see the references to specific government publications and statistics.

What to the numbers show? The numerical analysis demonstrates that we can afford the transition from the current pay-as-you-go Social Security system to a funded, two-tier system. In my judgment, the numbers show that the system we *cannot* afford is the current system.

What the Numbers Don't Show

I in no way claim that this analysis shows that mine is the only way to establish a funded Social Security system. This is only one way. My plan opens the door for new and different approaches. The concept, not the specific system, is the important issue. All suggestions for improvements and refinements are welcome.

I have been painstaking in seeking to prepare the most nearly complete and most detailed analysis I could. The analysis has been reviewed over and over for possible errors and tiny miscalculations. In spite of all these efforts, there may be some as-yet undiscovered error in my calculations. I recognize this possibility and make no claim to the contrary.

That notwithstanding, the foundation is firm and incontrovertible. For individuals setting aside income in a funded personal investment and retirement account, the capital accumulation over the years will be very substantial—well beyond most people's dreams. There is no doubt that trillions of dollars will be accumulating in individual savings in a mature, funded system.

I created a special model. I began with 100 million workers, all starting in the same year and all ending after forty-five years. With 100 million participating workers, after forty-five years Social Security benefits are $1.24 trillion. Only $260 billion are required from federal payroll taxes. The remainder comes from individual income from capital—an annual taxpayer saving of $980 billion. These numbers can go up or down with expected fluctuations in investment rates of return. But the numbers paint a picture, and the picture won't change. We can cut taxes and increase benefits.

BASIC FORMULAS UNDERLYING THE SYSTEM

1. Capital Growth and Compound Interest

Capital growth is calculated for four different set-aside levels:

$ 500 a year
$1,560 a year
$2,500 a year
$3,000 a year

Each set-aside increases each year 4 percent for inflation and 1 percent for real wage growth—i.e., a 5 percent per year increase. Following normal employment pay periods, the assumption is that deposits will be made twenty-six times per year (biweekly) to the individual savings and retirement accounts.

The capital growth is calculated at 8 percent interest per year, compounded quarterly. The accumulated capital amount is then reduced for inflation at a 4 percent per year rate to calculate the value of the money in the portfolio in constant (today's) dollars.

The average amount of capital deposited in each account each year is $1,274 as explained in the "Major Questions and Answers" section (following the present section). This is used to determine the annual accumulated capital and then the annual 5 percent income from capital.

2. Social Security Benefit Levels

At my request the Social Security Administration worked with Fiscal Associates, a Washington, D.C., consulting company which specializes in Social Security and entitlements, to determine the Social Security benefit levels.

The benefit levels are based on a 1996 worker who works forty-five years, and retires at age sixty-five—at year end 2040. The Social Security Administration reviewed these numbers and recommended adjustments, and Fiscal Associates made the corrections, which were then approved by the Social Security Administration.

On the basis of these numbers, Fiscal Associates has computerized all assumed salary levels. From the figures for salary at retirement, based on a retirement in 2040, the benefits are brought back to 1996 dollars.

We can enter the individual's salary levels ($10,000/year, $26,000/year, any number), the years that the individual participates in the system (one year through ten or twenty or forty-five, any number), and find the proper benefit levels.

MAJOR QUESTIONS AND ANSWERS: TIER 2 FUNDED SYSTEM

The following is an explanation of how much money is set aside into personal investment and retirement accounts and how much income is earned from capital. The numbers presented in this section include very slight variations due to rounding.

Question 1

In creating the proposed plan, how do we calculate: Who will participate and at what salary levels? How much money per year will be set aside into individual investment and retirement accounts? How much money will come from the Social Security system each year?

Answer

See the following analysis.

I made "reasonable person" estimates based on the different salary levels, to determine the personal savings matches and the likely level of participation within each salary level.

Analysis of account sizes:

There are 100.1 million workers participating in Tier 2 personal accounts. (Total workers number 125.3 million, and 25.2 million workers pay under $500 to Social Security.)

- **Average Government Set-aside (per person)**
  $99.165 billion divided by 100.1 million participants equals an average account of $991. This figure measures Social Security set-asides taken out of the system.
- **Average Total Portfolio (per person)**
  $127.468 billion divided by 100.1 million participants equals an average account of $1,274. This figure measures the average amount of capital deposited in each account each year.

Table A.1 Total Individuals Participating in Tier 2 Set-Asides Average Government Set-asides and Average Total Portfolio

Total participating workers (millions)	Average Social Security set-aside ($)	Tax-payer match ($)	Total port-folio ($)	Average total government ($ millions)	Average total portfolio ($ millions)
(1) 7.475	622	—	622	7.475 mil. workers × $622	7.475 mil. workers × $622
				$4,649	$4,649
(2) 30.230	500	—	500	30.230 mil. workers × $500	30.230 mil. workers × $500
				$15,115	$15,115
(3) 62.357	1,273	454	1,727	62.357 mil. workers × $1,273	62.357 mil. workers × $1,727
				$79,401	$107,704
100.1				$99,165	$127,468

Question 2

Of the 125.3 million total wage earners, how many do not participate in the funded Social Security system? How many workers pay less than $500 per year into Social Security?

Answer

A worker earning $4,032 per year pays $500 to Social Security. **1.** 23,539,000 workers earn $1–$3,599. They remain in the regular Tier 1 pay-as-you-go Social Security. They do not participate in Tier 2. In an operating, funded system, all workers, regardless of salary, will participate. There will not be a $4,032 minimum level. This is important for these purposes, because very few people have lifetime salaries of $4,032 and under. **2.** 18,346,000 workers earn $3,600–$8,399. 1.7 million—9 percent—earn less than $4,032 and do not participate in Tier 2. 16.6 million—91 percent—earn $4,032 or more, and do participate.

8,399	8,399	
− 3,600	− 4,032	4,367
$ 4,799	$4,367	4,799 = 91%

3. Of the 125.3 million total workers, 25.2 million do not participate in Tier 2. (See Question 6) They remain in Tier 1 and receive benefits as promised.

Question 3

Taxpayers earning $4,032 up to $5,999 are allowed to set aside all their Social Security taxes into personal accounts without a taxpayer savings match. How many taxpayers are in this group?

Answer

In the wage category of $3,600—$8,399 there are 18.346 million workers. 1.7 million earn below $4,032 and do not participate in Tier 2. 9.171 million earn $6,000–$8,399, calculated as follows:

8,399	8,399	
− 3,600	− 6,000	2,399
$ 4,799	$2,399	4,799 = 50%

        18.346 million total
     − 1.700 million Tier 1 only
     − 9.171 million requiring a savings match

Total: 7.475 million Tier 2 participants with no taxpayer savings match.

Question 4

How do we arrive at the average Social Security set-aside for these 7.475 million workers?

Answer

- 12.4% of $4,032: $500
- 12.4% of $5,999: $744
- Total set-aside: $1,244
- $1,244 divided by 2 equals an average set-aside of $622.
- Total annual set-aside is $4.649 billion. See (1) in Table A.1.

Question 5

Individuals earning $6,000 and above include a voluntary taxpayer savings match in order to receive a full Social Security set-aside beyond a $500 automatic set-aside. How does the taxpayer savings match work? How many workers participate and at what levels?

Answer

To set aside $1,560 into a personal investment and retirement account, individuals receive an automatic $500 set-aside from tax money they are already paying. To receive additional set-asides into their personal accounts, individuals set aside a voluntary after-tax savings match.

The savings match is on a sliding scale depending on wage level. The match begins at .43 of 1 percent of wage—$26 per year ($.50 per week) for individuals earning $6,000, and increases to a cap of 1.11 percent—$550 per year ($10.57 per week) for individuals earning $50,000 per year and over. The savings match caps at $550 per year. Individuals earning under $6,000 per year have no match requirement.

As an example, individuals earning $15,000 pay $1,860 into Social Security (employer and employee share). They receive an automatic deposit of $500 into their personal investment and retirement accounts.

If workers match $182 of savings, Social Security will set aside an additional $878 into their personal account for a total of $1,560. The remaining dollars above the $1,560 go to pay the Tier 1 pay-as-you-go obligations.

An analysis of the savings match at various salary ranges is presented in Table A.2.

Question 6

The taxpayer savings match is voluntary. How many workers will choose to participate? How many workers will choose not to participate?

Table A.2 Taxpayer Savings Match by Salary Range

Salary range ($)	Match as % of Wage	$ per year	Automatic set-aside ($)	Taxpayer match ($)	Soc. Sec. match ($)	Total set-aside ($)
0–5,999	0	0	No match required.			
6,000	.0043	26	500	26	218	744
7,500	.0069	52	500	52	378	930
8,400	.0092	78	500	78	463	1,041
10,000	.0130	130	500	130	610	1,240
12,580	.0124	156	500	156	904	1,560
15,000	.0121	182	500	182	878	1,560
17,500	.0118	208	500	208	852	1,560
20,000	.0117	234	500	234	826	1,560
22,250	.0116	260	500	260	800	1,560
25,000	.0114	286	500	286	774	1,560
27,500	.0113	312	500	312	748	1,560
30,000	.0112	338	500	338	722	1,560
32,500	.0112	364	500	364	696	1,560
35,000	.0111	390	500	390	670	1,560
37,500	.0110	416	500	416	644	1,560
40,000	.0110	442	500	442	618	1,560
42,500	.0110	468	500	468	592	1,560
45,000	.0109	494	500	494	566	1,560
47,500	.0109	520	500	520	540	1,560
50,000[a]	.0110	550	500	550	510	1,560

Note: To determine the voluntary taxpayer savings matches at each salary level, I made "reasonable person" estimates.
a. For $50,000 and over there is a taxpayer savings match cap at $550.

Answer

There are different assumed participation rates at each different income level. Individuals with salaries of $4,032–$5,999 are not required to participate in the savings match. At salaries of $6,000 and above, the participation rate generally increases as the salary level increases. A 50 percent participation rate is projected for the salary level $6,000–$8,399, and a 90 percent participation rate for $53,400 and above. These percentages are based on a total pool of 92.587 million workers—of whom 62.357 million participate. See Table A.3 for a detailed breakdown of participation rates.

Table A.3 Voluntary Taxpayer Savings Match
Participation Rates by Income Level

Earned salary ($)	Total workers (millions)	Percentage participation	Workers not participating (millions)	Workers participating (millions)
4,032–5,999	—	No match required.	—	—
6,000–8,399	9.171	50	4.586	4.585
8,400–13,199	16.039	65	5.614	10.425
13,200–17,999	14.420	65	5.047	9.373
18,000–22,799	12.250	65	4.287	7.963
22,800–27,599	9.709	65	3.398	6.311
27,600–32,399	7.515	70	2.254	5.261
32,400–37,199	5.859	70	1.758	4.101
37,200–41,999	4.432	70	1.330	3.102
42,000–46,799	3.211	75	.803	2.408
46,800–53,399	3.091	85	.464	2.627
53,400 and over	6.890	90	.689	6.201
Totals	92.587		30.230	62.357

Note: To determine participation rates at each salary level, I made "reasonable person" estimates.

Question 7

What benefits are available to workers who choose not to participate in the voluntary savings match?

Answer

There is an automatic $500 per year Social Security set-aside for individuals earning $4,032 and over who choose not to participate in the savings match. Assuming that 30.230 million workers will not participate in the savings match results in Social Security set-asides of $15.115 billion. See (2) in Table A.1.

Question 8

Individuals may set aside up to $3,000 per year into their Social Security Tier 2 account. How does this work? How many individuals will participate and at what levels?

Answer

Individuals will benefit by setting aside more than $1,560 in personal accounts because monies in Social Security Tier 2 accounts provide secure retirement income and may be passed tax-free to heirs or designees.

The government will also benefit because Social Security benefits will be paid without Tier 1 tax burdens. Social Security will not be means tested, but instead will become a capital accumulation program for over 100 million Americans.
Level 1—An additional $940 Set-Aside for a Total of $2,500:
If individuals wish to set aside an additional $940 in their personal Social Security accounts, they match $626 of after-tax savings, and Social Security sets aside an additional $314. The original set-aside is $1,560 plus $940 ($314 Social Security and $626 taxpayer savings) totaling $2,500.
Level 2—An Additional $500 Set-Aside for a Total of $3,000:
If individuals wish to set aside an additional $500 to raise their Tier 2 account to a maximum of $3,000 per year, they may. In Level 2, individuals are allowed to set aside $1,500 of their existing Social Security tax payments into their Tier 2 account matched by $1,500 of personal savings.
The following assumptions are used to determine participation in Level 1 and Level 2 additional set-asides:

Participation in Level 1 and Level 2 Additional Set-asides by Salary Range

Salary Range ($)	Percentage participation Level 1 $940 match (set-aside $2,500)	Percentage participation Level 2 $500 set-aside (set-aside $3,000)
27,599 and under	none	none
27,600–32,399	20	5
32,400–37,199	25	10
37,200–41,999	30	15
42,000–46,799	35	25
46,800–53,399	40	35
53,400–59,999	35	50
60,000 and over	30	60

Question 9
How many workers participate in the savings match? What is the average amount of capital deposited in each account each year?

Answer
See Question 6, which shows that 62.357 million workers participate in the taxpayer savings match. These calculations require a two-step process as follows.
Step One:
For each salary bracket, calculate an average individual taxpayer set-aside and an average individual Social Security match.

Table A.4   Numbers of Wage Earners Participating in Level 1 and Level 2 Set-asides (millions of persons)

Salary Range ($)	Total workers	Number participating in match	Number, regular match ($1,560)	Number, level 1 $940 match ($2,500)	Number, level 2 $500 match ($3,000)
27,600–32,399	7.515	5.261	3.946	1.052	.263
32,400–37,199	5.859	4.101	2.665	1.025	.411
37,200–41,999	4.432	3.102	1.706	.931	.465
42,000–46,799	3.211	2.408	.963	.843	.602
46,800–53,399	3.091	2.627	.657	1.051	.919
53,400–59,999	3.450	3.105	.466	1.087	1.552
60,000 and over	3.440	3.096	.310	.929	1.857
Totals	30.998	23.700	10.713	6.918	6.069

Multiply the number of participating workers in each salary bracket by the appropriate taxpayer match and the appropriate Social Security match.

Taxpayer matches and Social Security matches are calculated at three different levels: base (up to $1,560), Level 1 (up to $2,500), and Level 2 (up to $3,000). The taxpayer matches and the Social Security matches in each salary bracket are shown in Table A.5.

A summary of the data in Table A.1(3) is as follows:

- $28.303 billion divided by 62.357 million workers equals a $454 average taxpayer match.
- $79.401 billion divided by 62.357 million workers equals a $1,273 average Social Security match.
- $107.704 billion divided by 62.357 million workers equals a $1,727 average amount of capital deposited in each account each year.

ANNUAL DOLLAR VOLUME FOR TIER 2 SET-ASIDE: SOURCES AND BASIS OF NUMBERS

The following steps combine to determine the amount of money that Social Security will use from existing taxes to set aside each year in the personal investment and retirement accounts under the funded Tier 2 system. This measures the amount of money to be made up during the transition.

Table A.5 Taxpayer, Social Security Matches by Salary Bracket

Salary bracket ($)	Number of workers participating (millions)	Individual taxpayer matches ($)	Total taxpayer match (billions)	Individual Social Security matches ($)	Total Social Security match ($ billions)
6,000–8,399	4.585	52	.238	500 + 340 = 840	3.851
8,400–13,199	10.425	120	1.251	500 + 680 = 1,180	12.301
13,200–17,999	9.373	187	1.753	500 + 873 = 1,373	12.869
18,000–22,799	7.963	238	1.895	500 + 822 = 1,322	10.527
22,800–27,599	6.311	288	1.818	500 + 772 = 1,272	8.028
27,600–32,399	5.261				
Base (1,560)	3.946	337	1.330	500 + 723 = 1,223	4.826
Level 1	1.052	337 + 626 = 963	1.013	1,223 + 314 = 1,537	1.617
Level 2	.263	737 + 763 = 1,500	.394	1,500	.394
32,400–37,199	4.101				
Base (1,560)	2.665	386	1.029	500 + 674 = 1,174	3.129
Level 1	1.025	386 + 626 = 1,012	1.037	1,174 + 314 = 1,488	1.525
Level 2	.411	786 + 714 = 1,500	.616	1,500	.616
37,200–41,999	3.102				
Base (1,560)	1.706	436	.744	500 + 624 = 1,124	1.917
Level 1	.931	436 + 626 = 1,062	.989	1,124 + 314 = 1,438	1.339
Level 2	.465	836 + 664 = 1,500	.697	1,500	.697

(continued on next page)

Table A.5 (continued)

Salary bracket ($)	Number of workers participating (millions)	Individual taxpayer matches ($)	Total taxpayer match (billions)	Individual Social Security matches ($)	Total Social Security match ($ billions)
42,000–46,799	2.408				
Base (1,560)	.963	486	.468	500 + 574 = 1,074	1.034
Level 1	.843	486 + 626 = 1,112	.937	1,074 + 314 = 1,388	1.170
Level 2	.602	886 + 614 = 1,500	.903	1,500	.903
46,800–53,399	2.627				
Base (1,560)	.657	530	.348	500 + 530 = 1,030	.677
Level 1	1.051	530 + 626 = 1,156	1.215	1,030 + 314 = 1,344	1.412
Level 2	.919	930 + 570 = 1,500	1.378	1,500	1.378
53,400–59,999	3.105				
Base (1,560)	.466	550	.256	500 + 510 = 1,010	.471
Level 1	1.087	550 + 626 = 1,176	1.278	1,010 + 314 = 1,324	1.439
Level 2	1.552	950 + 550 = 1,500	2.328	1,500	2.328
60,000 and over	3.096				
Base (1,560)	.929	550	.511	500 + 510 = 1,010	.938
Level 1	.929	550 + 626 = 1,176	1.092	1,010 + 314 = 1,324	1.230
Level 2	1.857	950 + 550 = 1,500	2.785	1,500	2.785
Totals	62.357		28.303		79.401

Total portfolio: $107.704 billion

1. Calculate the number of U.S. workers.
2. Multiply total workers by 80 percent—the percentage of the workforce participating in Tier 2 (i.e., 80 percent of the workforce pays $500 and over into Social Security.) See Question 2 of the "Major Questions and Answers" section of the Appendix.
3. Multiply this number by $991—the average Social Security/government set-aside per year. See "Analysis of Account Sizes" under Question 1 of the "Major Questions and Answers" section of this Appendix.
4. Adjust each year for 1 percent real wage growth. Multiply the 1996 constant dollars by the appropriate raising power for each year.

The government sources for the data are as follows:

1. The U.S. population is found in the 1994 Social Security Trustees' Report, p. 144.

2. The number of U.S. workers is taken from the 1994 Social Security Trustees' Report, p. 119. The workers are listed every five years, from 1995 to 2040. The intervening years are calculated by subtracting the five-year difference and then dividing by five to obtain the per year increase.

3. The 1994 *Annual Statistical Supplement to the Social Security Bulletin,* Table 4.B7, p. 173 breaks down the 1991 wage and salary workers by income groups. This table is used to determine how many workers pay $500 and over to Social Security.

In 1991 there were an additional 7,500,000 self-employed workers. The assumption is that their income spread is proportional to wage and salary workers.

4. The total analysis of workforce in "Analysis of Account Sizes," under Question 1 in the Appendix section "Major Questions and Answers" calculates the average government set-aside as $991.

5. The appropriate raising power for each year is provided by the Office of the Actuary at national Social Security.

Existing Payroll Taxes Set Aside by Social Security into Funded Accounts

The projected set-asides, beginning in 1996, are shown in Table A.6.

Income from Capital

The following steps determine how much capital is accumulated and how much income from capital is received by Social Security beneficiaries:

Calculate the Average Portfolio

Please see "Analysis of Account Sizes" in Question 1. The average amount of capital deposited in each account each year is $1,274.

Table A.6 Total U.S. Workers, Number of Participating Workers in Tier 2 Set-aside, Savings/Set-aside

	U.S. population (millions)	U.S. workers (millions)	Tier 2 workers (80% of workforce)	Savings/ set-aside at $991 average (billions)	Raising power (1% real wage)	Tier 2 annual set-aside personal accounts[a] (billions)
1996	275.6	140.6	112.5	111.5	—	111.5
1997		142.0	113.6	112.6	1.009	113.6
1998		143.5	114.8	113.8	1.019	115.9
1999		145.0	116.0	115.0	1.029	118.3
2000	285.0	146.5	117.2	116.1	1.039	120.7
2001		147.7	118.2	117.1	1.049	122.9
2002		149.0	119.2	118.1	1.059	125.1
2003		150.2	120.2	119.1	1.069	127.3
2004		151.4	121.1	120.0	1.079	129.5
2005	295.6	152.6	122.1	121.0	1.089	131.8
2006		153.6	122.9	121.8	1.100	134.0
2007		154.5	123.6	122.5	1.111	136.1
2008		155.5	124.1	123.0	1.121	137.9
2009		156.5	125.1	124.0	1.132	140.3
2010	305.9	157.4	125.9	124.8	1.143	142.6
2011		157.9	126.3	125.2	1.154	144.4
2012		158.4	126.7	125.6	1.165	146.3
2013		158.9	127.1	126.0	1.176	148.1
2014		159.4	127.5	126.3	1.187	150.0
2015	315.9	159.9	127.9	126.7	1.199	152.0
2016		160.1	128.1	126.9	1.210	153.6
2017		160.4	128.3	127.1	1.222	155.4
2018		160.6	128.5	127.3	1.234	157.1
2019		160.8	128.6	127.4	1.246	158.8
2020	325.0	161.0	128.8	127.6	1.258	160.6
2021		161.1	128.9	127.7	1.270	162.2
2022		161.3	129.0	127.8	1.282	163.9
2023		161.4	129.1	127.9	1.294	165.5
2024		161.6	129.2	128.0	1.307	167.3
2025	333.0	161.7	129.4	128.2	1.319	169.1
2026		161.9	129.5	128.3	1.332	170.9
2027		162.2	129.7	128.5	1.345	172.9
2028		162.4	129.9	128.7	1.358	174.8
2029		162.6	130.1	128.9	1.371	176.8
2030	339.5	162.8	130.2	129.0	1.384	178.6

(continued on next page)

2031		163.1	130.5	129.3	1.397	180.7
2032		163.5	130.7	129.5	1.411	182.7
2033		163.8	131.0	129.8	1.424	184.9
2034		164.1	131.3	130.1	1.438	187.1
2035	344.6	164.4	131.5	130.3	1.452	189.2
2036		164.8	131.8	130.6	1.466	191.5
2037		165.1	132.1	130.9	1.480	193.7
2038		165.4	132.3	131.1	1.494	195.9
2039		165.7	132.5	131.3	1.509	198.1
2040	348.5	166.0	132.8	131.6	1.523	200.4
2041		166.2	133.0	131.8	1.538	202.7
2042		166.4	133.1	131.9	1.553	204.9
2043		166.7	133.4	132.2	1.568	207.2
2044		166.9	133.5	132.3	1.583	209.5
2045	351.5	167.1	133.7	132.5	1.598	211.7
2046		167.2	133.8	132.6	1.614	213.9
2047		167.3	133.8	132.6	1.629	216.1
2048		167.5	134.0	132.8	1.645	218.4
2049		167.6	134.1	132.9	1.661	220.7
2050	354.1	167.7	134.2	132.9	1.677	223.0
2051		167.8	134.2	133.0	1.693	225.2
2052		167.9	134.3	133.1	1.709	227.5
2053		167.9	134.3	133.1	1.725	229.6
2054		168.0	134.4	133.2	1.742	232.0
2055	356.5	168.1	134.5	133.3	1.759	234.4
2056		168.2	134.6	133.4	1.776	236.9
2057		168.3	134.6	133.4	1.793	239.2
2058		168.4	134.7	133.5	1.810	241.6
2059		168.5	134.8	133.6	1.827	244.1
2060	359.0	168.6	134.9	133.7	1.845	246.6
2061		168.7	135.0	133.7	1.863	249.2
2062		168.8	135.0	133.8	1.881	251.7
2063		168.9	135.1	133.9	1.899	254.3
2064		169.0	135.2	134.0	1.917	256.8
2065	361.6	169.1	135.3	134.1	1.935	259.4
2066		169.2	135.4	134.1	1.954	262.1
2067		169.3	135.4	134.2	1.973	264.8
2068		169.4	135.5	134.3	1.992	267.5
2069		169.5	135.6	134.4	2.010	270.1
2070	364.1	169.6	135.7	134.5	2.030	273.0

a. These figures are obtained by multiplying the cost of savings/set-aside by the raising power.

Sources: Federal Old-Age and Survivors Insurance and Disability Insurance Trust Fund (OASDI), Board of Trustees, *1994 Annual Report,* House Document 103–231 (Washington, D.C.: U.S. Government Printing Office, April 12, 1994) for U.S. population. Number of U.S. workers and number of Tier 2 workers found in Social Security Administration, Office of Research and Statistics, *Annual Statistical Supplement, 1994, to the Social Security Bulletin,* SSA Publication no. 13-11700 (Washington, D.C.: U.S. Department of Health and Human Services, August 1994), 173. Cost of savings/set-aside calculated in "Major Questions and Answers" section, Question 1, of the Appendix. Raising power from Social Security long-term actuaries in the Office of the Actuary at national Social Security.

Calculate the Percentage of Beneficiaries Who Are Workers

The 1994 Social Security Trustees' Report (pp. 156, 161) breaks out total beneficiaries into workers, auxiliaries, dependents, and disabled workers. For 1995, workers are listed as 70.9 percent of total beneficiaries. By 2070, workers are projected to be 85.3 percent of beneficiaries. Assume that an acceptable average is that 80 percent of beneficiaries are workers.

Calculate the Percentage of Workers Who Are Disabled

The 1994 Social Security Trustees' Report (pp. 156, 161) lists disabled workers as 13.8 percent of all workers in 1995, 18.6 percent in 2010, and 15.1 percent in 2020, descending to 11.4 percent in 2070. Assume that 14.2 percent of workers are disabled, as an average.

Calculate the Percentage of Capital Received as Income

All individuals retain the right to create an annuity with 100 percent of their capital, and deplete all the capital by their death and the death of their spouses. The following formulas and assumptions were used to calculate the annuity rates.

- Assume an average eighteen-year life expectancy. Assume an ongoing capital growth of 8 percent—4 percent in constant dollars.
- On $100,000:
  Present Value = $100,000
  Future Value = $0
  Number of Years = 18
  Interest = 4 (constant dollars)
  Annual Payment = $7,899 per year or 7.9 percent

Individuals choosing an annuity can expect a 7.9 percent return on capital during their expected lifetimes.

The Social Security Administration statistics demonstrate that women are expected to live longer than men. For reasons of simplicity, 7.9 percent was selected to use as an average.

For an individual who wishes to retain the capital nest egg, and transfer the capital tax-free to his or her heirs, the assumption is a 5 percent annual income from capital.

As a rule of thumb, 5 percent interest income seems practical and reasonable. A majority of nonprofits and schools with endowments and individual trust beneficiaries use a 5 percent income guideline.

With a 5 percent interest income, it is understood that the capital base might lose partial value in constant 1996 dollars over an eighteen-year period.

Calculate Number of Years Worked and Average Years of Compounding Capital Accumulations

The Social Security Administration has provided me with worksheets—"Male Covered Worker Rates (per Hundred) and Female Covered Worker Rates (per Hundred)"—which show years 1992 through 2070 and include the number of workers per hundred that work for five-year periods from less than age twenty, to age seventy and over.

These charts become the basis of estimating the overall working lifetimes of workers, and the number of years of compounding capital accumulations.
Impact of Work Age Fifteen to Twenty:
More than seventy out of one hundred males and females under the age of twenty hold jobs. (Male: 1996: 74.24. 2006: 70.87. 2020: 68.5. Female: 1996: 73.01. 2006: 71.51. 2020: 69.48.)

All money earned from age fifteen to twenty, and compounded for fifty to fifty-five years substantially increases capital accumulations. These early set-asides add an extra cycle of compounded interest.
Impact of Work Age Sixty-five to Sixty-nine; Seventy to Seventy-nine:
These numbers show that over 30 percent of males age sixty-five to sixty-nine hold jobs. (1996: 36.24 percent. 2006: 19.06 percent.) Over 20 percent of females age sixty-five to sixty-nine hold jobs. (1996: 22.16. 2006: 20.65.) An esimated 19 percent of males and 8.5 percent of females age seventy to seventy-nine hold jobs. (1996: 19.76. 2006: 19.20.)

Compounding set-aside money for an extra five or ten years leads to a substantial increase in accumulated capital.
Impact of Compound Interest and Capital Ownership:
Under the proposed system, workers will see how compound interest works in their favor for every extra year of work. There will be a high incentive to work extra years. It is fair to assume that 15 to 20 percent of workers will work an extra three to five years to benefit from the substantial capital increases in the final years.

The current Social Security system creates built-in incentives for employees (especially those under twenty) and employers not to report income. The taxes are high, and money taken "off the books" increases an employee's disposable income by 6.2 percent.

The system based on capital accumulation creates totally opposite incentives. Employees will want to report income and set aside the dollars once they see the impact of compound interest on their economic independence.
Impact of Early Work and Pay-ins Compared with Later Work and Pay-ins:
The work patterns of both male and female workers show that the highest percentages of work performed occur from the years under twenty through age sixty. After age sixty, work patterns decline.

The impact of early work on compounding is beneficial. The early money doubles every seven to eight years. Pay-ins in the last few years have a small impact on the final capital accumulated.

Analysis of Existing Covered Worker Rates:

Another look at the Social Security Administration worksheets shows that the average male works forty-three and one-half years, and the average female works forty-one years. (Data based on sample year 2020 and current working ages.) These numbers also show that few people work uninterrupted for forty-five years. Spreading the work and contributing to set-asides over ten to fifteen additional years adds to capitalization.

Average Years of Work for Disabled Workers:

The Social Security tables indicate that disabled workers will accumulate less capital because they work an average of thirty-five years, less time than the average worker.

Summary and Impact on Capital Accumulations:

With the assistance of the Social Security Administration, the final "standard" worker income from capital assumption was reasonably selected.

Disabled workers show a substantial decrease in accumulated capital. The $1,274 compounded for thirty-five years totals $111,205. This is only 59.2 percent of the $187,780 accumulated after forty-five years.

Workers who are not disabled, because of compound interest calculations over extra years, are likely to have capital accumulations of forty-five years plus 11.988 percent, or 12 percent.

The average capital accumulation variation is found in the following calculations:

$$
\begin{array}{lr}
\$100 \times 14.2 \text{ disabled workers} \times .592 \text{ percent capital} = & 840.6 \\
\$100 \times 85.8 \text{ workers} \times 1.12 \text{ percent capital} = & \underline{9,609.6} \\
& 10,450.2
\end{array}
$$

The average accumulation variation is 1.045—a 4.5 percent increase.

Based on these assumptions, income from capital can be calculated as follows:

1. Multiply the number of beneficiaries in a given year by .80 to get the number of participating individuals in Tier 2 set-asides. Multiply again by .80 to get the number of workers. Divide this number by 18 to get the annual number of workers setting capital aside.

2. Calculate capital growth for an average set-aside of $1,274 per year for years 1 through 49. Take 5 percent of the capital base as annual income from capital and multiply this by 1.045.

3. Multiply the number of annual workers by the annual income and spread this number for 18 years. Total for each year.

MODEL I

The selected salary ranges in Table A.7 are taken directly from the Social Security Administration's 1994 *Statistical Supplement*. The benefit levels are the averages of the high and low salaries in each category.

MODEL II: A 100 PERCENT PARTICIPATION ALTERNATIVE FOR COMPARISON

After many months of discussing my proposed plan with numerous professionals, three recommendations emerged as the basis for a model that can serve as an alternative for comparison purposes.

First, the professionals wanted to see the impact if all working Americans participated fully. Under the original plan, 30 million Americans voluntarily opt to participate at the mandatory $500 set-aside level only and not to participate with the savings matches, which allow full capital accumulation. The basis of the model is 100 percent participation.

Second, the original plan had five set-aside levels—$500 (mandatory); $500 to $1,559 (wages of $4,032 to $12,579); $1,560, $2,500, and $3,000. The professionals wanted to see a more developed plan whereby the set-aside levels would increase as salaries increased (i.e., more set-aside levels, scaling up proportionately as salaries increase).

Table A.7   Model I Benefit Comparisons

	Existing pay-as-you-go system			Funded system		
	Present Law benefits	Likely future benefits with cuts	Benefits with annuity	5% Income from capital	Estate capital nest egg
Wages/salary					
$8,400–$13,199	$9,482	$8,323	$16,967	$10,738	$214,771
$22,800–$27,599	$15,979	$14,026	$20,345	$12,876	$257,527
$37,200–41,999	$21,124	$18,542	$32,604	$20,635	$412,704
$53,400–$60,000	$24,742	$21,707	$39,124	$24,762	$495,245

Estate capital nest egg
$0 in all cases

Note: the average per year set-aside assumptions are $1,300, $1,560, $2,500, and $3,000 respectively for each wage/salary category.

Third, the professionals felt that the original savings set-asides were too low. This alternative model increases the savings match levels. The original savings matches began at salaries of $6,000 at .43 percent of wage and built to 1.14 percent for wages of $25,000, and 2.5 percent for high-salary wages with a cap at a $3,000 per year set-aside.

The new savings matches include all wage levels and range from 1.5 percent for wages of $4,032 to $5,999 ($1.15 to $1.73 per week), to 2.0 percent for wages of $8,400 to $37,200 ($3.23 to $14.30 per week) to 2.5 percent for wages of $42,000 to $60,000 and over ($20.19 to $28.85 per week). (The maximum Social Security wage is $61,200.)

This alternative model demonstrates that many options are possible. There is no definitive plan. Readers and other professionals are invited to create different options.

The selected salary ranges in Table A.8 are taken directly from the Social Security Administration's 1994 *Statistical Supplement.* The benefit levels are the averages of the high and low salaries in each category.

The Model II assumptions create:

- Average portfolio: $1,564
  $156.58 billion total portfolio divided by 100.1 million participating workers equals an average portfolio size of $1,564.
- Average cost of government set-aside: $1,077
  $107.85 billion total Social Security payroll tax set-asides divided by 100.1 million participating workers equals an average government cost of the set-aside from payroll taxes of $1,077.

Table A.8   Model II Benefit Comparisons

| | Existing pay-as-you-go system | | | Funded system | |
| | | | | | |
Wages/salary	Present Law benefits	Likely future benefits with cuts	Benefits with annuity	5% Income from capital	Estate capital nest egg
$8,400–$13,199	$9,482	$8,323	$16,015	$10,136	$202,719
$22,800–$27,599	$15,979	$14,026	$23,474	$14,857	$297,146
$37,200–$41,999	$21,124	$18,542	$30,412	$19,248	$384,969
$53,400–$60,000	$24,742	$21,707	$37,853	$23,957	$479,149
	Estate capital nest egg $0 in all cases				

- Comparison with the original plan (Model I):
  The average total portfolio size in the original plan was $1,274. The average government cost of the set-aside from payroll taxes was $991.

  The total portfolio size of the comparison model increases for two main reasons: 30 million extra workers are fully participating, and the personal savings matches are increased. The average government cost of the set-aside from payroll taxes increases because an extra 30 million workers are fully participating.

Bibliography

Aaron, Henry J., Barry P. Bosworth, and Gary T. Burtless. *Can America Afford To Grow Old? Paying for Social Security.* Washington, D.C.: Brookings Institution, 1989.

Advisory Council on Social Security. "Financing (Funding) Approaches for Social Security Designed for 1994 Trustees Intermediate Assumptions." Paper prepared October 21, 1994, Washington, D.C.

————. "Financing (Funding) Approaches for Social Security Designed for 1994 Trustees Intermediate Assumptions." Paper prepared February 7, 1995, Washington, D.C.

————. *Interim Report on Social Security and the Federal Budget.* Deborah Steelman chairwoman. Washington, D.C., July, 1990.

————. *Social Security Financing and Benefits.* Report, Henry J. Aaron chairman. Washington, D.C., 1979.

Agar, Herbert, and Allen Tate. *Who Owns America?* Boston: Houghton Mifflin, 1986.

American Association of Retired Persons. *A Guide to Understanding Your Pension Plan: A Pension Handbook.* National Pension Assistance Project, AARP. Washington, D.C., 1989.

American Enterprise Institute. *Private Pensions and the Public Interest: A Symposium.* Washington, D.C., 1970.

American Federation of Labor and Congress of Industrial Organizations. *Pension-Net Conference: Selected Speeches.* AFL-CIO Department of Employee Benefits. Washington, D.C., 1992.

Andrews, Emily S. *Pension Policy and Small Employers: At What Price Coverage?* Employee Benefit Research Institute Education and Research Fund. Washington, D.C., 1989.

Association of Private Pension and Welfare Plans. *Gridlock: On the Road toward Pension Simplification.* Washington, D.C., September, 1991.

————. *National Retirement Income Policy.* Washington, D.C., June 1992.

————. *Why We Should Not Tax Employee Benefits.* Washington, D.C., May, 1990.

————. *25 Years Of Excellence: 1967–1992.* Washington, D.C., 1993.

Ball, David George. "President's Agenda for Pensions and Health Benefits. "Speech delivered before the Southwest Area Commerce and Industry Association, Greenwich, Conn., September 23, 1992.

Barber, Randy, and Jeremy Rifkin. *The North Will Rise Again: Pensions, Politics and Power in the 1980s.* Boston: Beacon Press, 1978.

Beller, Daniel J., and John A. Turner, eds. *Trends in Pensions 1992.* U.S. Department of Labor Pension and Welfare Administration. Washington, D.C.: U.S. Government Printing Office, 1992.

Bernstein, Merton. *The Future of Private Pensions.* London: Free Press of Glencove,1964.

Bipartisan Commission on Entitlement and Tax Reform. *Final Report to the President,* J. Robert Kerrey chairman, John C. Danforth vice-chairman. Washington, D.C.: U.S. Government Printing Office, 1995.

Boeker, Paul H. "Developing Strong Capital Markets: Contrasting Latin American and East Asian Experience." Paper presented at the Second Hemisphere Conference on Social Security, Pension Reform, and Capital Markets Development. The Inter-American Development Bank and the Institute of the Americas, Washington, D.C., June, 1995.

Bogle, John. *Bogle on Mutual Funds.* New York: Richard D. Irwin, Inc., 1994.

Borden, Karl. "Dismantling the Pyramid: The Way and How of Privatizing Social Security." Unpublished manuscript. University of Nebraska, Omaha, 1994.

Bosworth, Barry. "The Social Security Fund: How Big? How Managed?" Paper prepared for the Brookings Institution, January 1995.

Bosworth, Barry, Rudiger Dornbusch, and Raul Laban. *The Chilean Economy: Policy Lessons and Challenges.* Washington, D.C.: Brookings Institution, 1994.

Brooke, James. "Quiet Revolution in Latin Pensions." *New York Times,* September 10, 1994, Business, 1.

Bureau of the Census. *Current Population Survey: Income, Poverty and Valuation of Noncash Benefits.* Consumer Income Series. Washington, D.C.: U.S. Department of Commerce, March 1994.

————. *Historical Statistics of the United States: Colonial Times to 1970.* Washington, D.C.: U.S. Department of Commerce, 1975.

Burkhauser, Richard V., and Dallas L. Salisbury, eds. *Pensions in a Changing Economy.* Employee Benefit Research Institute and National Academy on Aging. Washington, D.C., 1993.

Burns, James MacGregor. *A People's Charter: The Pursuit of Rights in America.* New York: Alfred A. Knopf, 1991.

Bush, George. *Agenda for American Renewal.* Bush-Quayle '92 General Committee. Washington, D.C., 1992.

Canfield, Anne C. and Stuart J. Sweet. "Enhancing Retirement Security: A Proposal." Statement at Hearings on S. 2016, Committee on Finance, U.S. Senate, February 5, 8, 27, 1990.

————. "Sweet/Canfield 1994 Social Security Plan." Testimony before the Subcommittee on Social Security, Committee on Ways and Means, U.S. House of Representatives, October 4, 1994.

Carman, Harry J., Harold C. Syrett, and Bernard W. Wishy, eds. *A History of the American People.* Vol. 1. New York: Alfred A. Knopf, 1960.

Central Provident Fund Board. *CPF Members' Handbook.* Singapore, April 1985.

Chambers, Letitia, and James A. Rotherham. *Social Security Financing.* Monograph Series. National Committee to Preserve Social Security and Medicare. Washington, D.C., July 25, 1994.

Citizens for Tax Justice. *A Far Cry from Fair: CTJ's Guide to State Tax Reform.* Washington, D.C., April 1991.

————. *1991: CTJ's Year in Review.* Washington, D.C., 1992.

Commerce News. U.S. Department of Commerce, Washington, D.C. September 29, 1994.

Committee on Ways and Means, U.S. House of Representatives. *1994 Green Book: Overview of Entitlement Programs.* Washington, D.C.: U.S. Government Printing Office, July 15, 1994.

Concord Coalition. *The Zero Deficit Plan: A Plan for Eliminating the Federal Budget Deficit by the Year 2000.* Washington, D.C., 1994.

Congressional Research Service. *Joint Pension Trusteeship: Analysis of the Visclosky Proposal.* Washington, D.C., 1990.

Darnell, Tim. *The Pension Pot of Gold? American City and County Magazine,* November, 1987.

Deaton, Richard Lee. *The Political Economy of Pensions, Power Politics, and Social Change.* Vancouver: University of British Columbia Press, 1989.

Declaration of Independence. In *A History of the American People.* Vol. 1, ed. Harry J. Carman, Harold C. Syrett, and Bernard W. Wishy, appendix I, 759. New York: Alfred A. Knopf, 1960.

Dixon, Jennifer. "Poll Finds Young Americans Doubt Social Security Future." *Washington Post,* Tuesday, September 27, 1994, sec. C, 1.

Downs, Christopher J., and Rosalind Stevens-Strohmann. "Providing Fair Pensions Efficiently." *Risk, Insurance and Welfare Report by the Association of British Insurers.* London, 1995.

Drucker, Peter. "Reckoning with the Pension Fund Revolution." *Harvard Business Review,* March/April 1991.

————. *The Unseen Revolution.* New York: Harper and Row, 1976.

EBRI-ERF Policy Forum. *America in Transition: Benefits for the Future.* Employee Benefit Research Institute Education and Research Fund. Washington, D.C., 1987.

————. *Business, Work, and Benefits: Adjusting to Change.* Employee Benefit Research Institute Education and Research Fund. Washington, D.C., 1989.

Economic Report of the President. Transmitted to the Congress February 1995. Washington, D.C.: U.S. Government Printing Office.

Employee Benefit Research Institute. *Employment-based Retirement Income Benefits: Analysis of the 1993 Current Population Survey Supplement.* Employee Benefit Research Institute Education and Research Fund. Washington, D.C., 1994.

————. *Fundamentals of Employee Benefit Programs.* 4th ed. Employee Benefit Research Institute Education and Research Fund. Washington, D.C., 1990.

————. *Pension Investments and Financial Markets.* Issue Brief no. 80. Washington, D.C., 1988.

Entin, Stephen J. "Reforming Social Security In a Pro-Growth Manner." Prepared statement before the Subcommittee on Social Security, Committee on Ways and Means. Institute for Research on the Economics of Taxation (IRET), Washington, D.C., September 7, 1994.

————. "Summary of Statement before Committee on Ways and Means Hearing on the Senior Citizens' Equity Act: Reforming Taxation of Social Security Benefits." Institute for Research on the Economics of Taxation (IRET), Washington, D.C., January 19, 1995.

————. "Summary of Statement before Subcommittee on Social Security of the Committee on Ways and Means Hearing on the Senior Citizens' Equity Act." Institute for Research on the Economics of Taxation (IRET), Washington, D.C.: January 9, 1995.

Farkas, Steve, and Jean Johnson. *Promises to Keep: How Leaders and the Public Respond to Saving and Retirement.* A Report from Public Agenda in Collaboration with the Employee Benefit Research Institute. Washington, D.C., 1994.

Federal Hospital Insurance Trust Fund (HI), Board of Trustees. *1994 Annual Report.* Washington, D.C.: U.S. Government Printing Office, April 11, 1994.

Federal Old-Age and Survivors Insurance and Disability Insurance Trust Funds (OASDI), Board of Trustees. *1994 Annual Report.* House Document 103-231. Washington, D.C.: U.S. Government Printing Office, April 12, 1994.

Federal Supplementary Medical Insurance Trust Fund (SMI), Board of Trustees, *1994 Annual Report.* House Document 103-229. Washington, D.C.: U.S. Government Printing Office, April 12, 1994.

Fenner, Elizabeth. "A Lush 401(k)." *Money,* November 1992, 93.

Ferguson, Karen, and Kate Blackwell. *Pensions in Crisis: How the System is Failing America and How You Can Protect Your Future.* The Pension Rights Center. Arcade Publishing, Inc., New York: Little, Brown and Company, May 1995.

Ferrara, Peter J. *Social Security: The Inherent Contradiction.* Washington, D.C.: Cato Institute, 1980.

————, ed. *Social Security: Prospects for Real Reform.* Washington, D.C.: Cato Institute, 1985.

Foley, Jill D., and Joseph S. Pacentini. *EBRI Databook on Employee Benefits.* 2d ed. Employee Benefit Research Institute Education and Research Fund. Washington, D.C., 1992.

Franklin Technical Institute. *The Codicil of the Will of Benjamin Franklin*. Boston, 1965.

Ghilarducci, Teresa. *Labor's Capital: The Economics of Private Pensions*. Cambridge, Mass.: MIT Press 1992.

Goodman, John C., and Gerald L. Musgrave. *Patient Power: Solving America's Health Care Crisis*. Washington, D.C.: The Cato Institute, 1992.

Grad, Susan. *Income of the Population 55 or Older, 1992*. Social Security Administration, Office of Research and Statistics, SSA Publication no. 13-11871. Washington, D.C.: U.S. Department of Health and Human Services, May, 1994.

Greenough, William. *Pension Plans and Public Policy*. New York: Columbia University Press, 1976.

Gropper, Diane Hall. "When Dallas Talks, Washington Listens." *Institutional Investor,* November 1985.

Grubbs, Donald S., Jr. "MUPS and Portability: Prospects for the Future," Unpublished paper, Silver Spring, Md., May 15, 1981.

Henson, Mary. *Trends in the Income of Families and Persons in the U.S., 1947–64*. Bureau of the Census. Washington, D.C.: U.S. Department of Commerce, 1967.

Hidy, Ralph W., Muriel E. Hidy, and Roy V. Scott. *The Great Northern Railway: A History*. Boston: Harvard Business School Press, 1988.

Howe, Neil, and Richard Jackson. *1994 NTUF Chartbook on Entitlements and the Aging of America*. National Taxpayers Union Foundation. Washington, D.C., 1994.

Howe, Neil, and William Strauss. *Generations*. New York: William Morrow and Company, 1991.

Ibbotson Associates. "Stocks, Bonds, and Inflation." *1992 Yearbook: Market Results for 1926–1991*. Chicago, 1992.

Information Please Almanac. 47th ed. Boston and New York: Houghton Mifflin, 1994.

Institute for Fiduciary Education. *Economically Targeted Investments: A Reference for Public Pension Funds*. Sacramento, Calif., 1989.

Institute for Research on the Economics of Taxation. *Pay-As-You-Go Entitlements, the Baby-Boom, and the Federal Budget: Facing up to Reality*. IRET Policy Bulletin no. 64. Washington, D.C., November 7, 1994.

Investor Responsibility Research Center. *New Directions in the Investment and Control of Pension Funds*. Washington, D.C., 1983.

James, Estelle. *Averting the Old Age Crisis: An Overview*. Policies to Protect the Old and Promote Growth. Washington, D.C.: World Bank and Oxford University Press, 1995.

Kelly, Thomas W. *Wealth Is Not a Dirty Word*. Savers and Investors League, Savers and Investors Foundation. Paoli, Pa: Mill Run Press, 1994.

Kelso, Louis O. *The New Capitalist*. New York: Random House, 1961.

Kelso, Louis O. and Patricia Hetter. *Two-Factor Theory: The Economics of Reality*. New York: Vintage Books, 1968.

Kennickell, Arthur B., and Louise R. Woodburn. *Estimation of Household Net Worth Using Model-based and Design-based Weights: Evidence from the 1989 Survey of Consumer Finances*. Federal Reserve Board. Washington, D.C. April 1992.

Klugman, Mark M. *About the International Center for Pension Reform*. Santiago, Chile, 1995.

Kolko, Gabriel. *Wealth and Power in America: An Analysis of Social Class*. New York: Praeger 1964.

Koselka, Rita. "A Better Way to Do It." *Forbes,* October 28, 1991.

Kotlikoff, Laurence J. "The U.S. Fiscal and Saving Crises: The Role of Entitlements." Paper presented at the IRET Conference on Social Security and Business Costs, Washington, D.C. February 9, 1995.

Kotlikoff, Laurence J., Jagadeesh Gokhale, and John Sabelhaus. "Understanding the Postwar Decline in United States Saving: A Cohort Analysis." Paper presented at IRET Conference, Washington, D.C., Thursday, February 9, 1995.

Kotlikoff, Laurence, and Daniel Smith. *Pensions in the American Economy*. Chicago: University of Chicago Press, 1983.

Luntz, Frank, and Mark Siegel. *Social Security: The Credibility Gap*. Analysis of the Third Millennium Survey. New York: Third Millennium, September 1994.

Lynn, Robert J. *The Pension Crisis*. Lexington, Mass.: Lexington Books, 1983.

Maguire, Steven R. "Employer and Occupational Tenure: 1991 Update." *Monthly Labor Review*, June 1993, 45.

McFadden, John. *Retirement Plans for Employers*. Homewood, Ill.: Richard D. Irwin, 1988.

McGill, Dan M. *The Fundamentals of Private Pensions*. 5th ed., Pension Research Council, Wharton School of Business, University of Pennsylvania. Philadelphia, 1984.

McIntyre, Robert S. "Just Taxes and Other Options." Reprinted from *Less Taxing Alternatives*. Citizens for Tax Justice. Washington, D.C., March 1984.

McSteen, Martha. "Long-Term Solvency of Social Security and Adequacy and Equity in Benefits." Paper submitted to the 1994–1995 Advisory Council on Social Security. National Committee to Preserve Social Security and Medicare. Washington, D.C., March 9, 1995.

Merrill Lynch. *Individual Retirement Accounts: Saving the American Dream*. New York, January 1995.

Miller, Herman. *Rich Man, Poor Man*. New York: Thomas Y. Crowell Company, 1971.

Millstein, Ira. "Can Pension Funds Lead the Ownership Revolution." *Harvard Business Review*, May–June, 1991, 166–183.

Moffett, Matt. "Latin American Model for Financial Reform." *Wall Street Journal*, August 22, 1994, 1.

Munn, James S. "Social Security Reform." Unpublished position paper, Seattle, Washington, May 1995.

Munnell, Alicia H. *The Economics of Private Pensions*. Washington, D.C.: Brookings Institution, 1982.

Nader, Ralph, and Kate Blackwell. *You and Your Pension*. New York: Grossman Publishers, 1973.

National Association of State Retirement Administrators. *Survey of State Retirement Systems*. Washington, D.C., 1976.

National Income and Products Accounting of the United States. Vol. 1, 1929–1958. Washington, D.C.: U.S. Government Printing Office, 1994.

Nevins, Allan. *Ford: The Times, The Man, The Company*. New York: Charles Scribner's Sons, 1954.

Perkins, Joseph. Statement by the American Society of Retired Persons before the 1994–1955 Advisory Council on Social Security. Washington, D.C., March 8, 1995.

Peterson, Peter G., and Neil Howe. *On Borrowed Time: How the Growth in Entitlement Spending Threatens America's Future*. San Francisco: ICS Press, 1988.

Piñera, José. "The Chilean Experience." Speech delivered at the Cato Institute Public Policy Forum, Washington, D.C., April 28, 1995.

President's Committee on Corporate Pension Funds. *Public Policy and Private Pension Programs*. Committee established by President Kennedy; final report presented to President Johnson. Washington, D.C., 1964.

Quinn, Jane Bryant. "Is Your Pension Fund Safe?" *Newsweek*, April 22, 1991.

Robbins, Gary, and Aldona Robbins. *Salvaging Social Security: The Incredible Shrinking Trust Fund, and What We Can Do about It.* IPI Policy Report no. 130. Lewisville, Tex.: Institute for Policy Innovation, April 1995.

Robertson, A. Haeworth. *Social Security: What Every Taxpayer Should Know.* Retirement Policy Institute. Washington, D.C., 1992.

Rossiter, Clinton. *Seedtime of the Republic.* New York: Harcourt, Brace, 1953.

Rother, John C. "Options for the Future." *Modern Maturity.* American Association of Retired Persons, Washington, D.C. July-August, 1995, 100.

Salisbury, Dallas L. Interview by Sam Beard. December 6, 1994.

Schmitt, Ray. *Minimum Universal Pension System (MUPS).* Congressional Research Service. Washington, D.C.: Library of Congress, 1987.

——— . *Pension Benefit Guarantee Corp.: Proposal to Shore Up the Single-Employer Program.* Congressional Research Service. Washington, D.C.: Library of Congress. 1992.

——— . *Pension Portability: What Does It Mean? How Does It Work?* Congressional Research Service, Washington, D.C.: Library of Congress. 1988.

——— . *Private Pension Issues.* Congressional Research. Washington, D.C.: Library of Congress. 1991.

——— . *Private Pension Plan Standards. A Summary of ERISA.* Congressional Research Service. Washington, D.C.: Library of Congress. 1990.

Schmitt, Ray, Carolyn Merk, and Jennifer Neisman, *Public Pension Plans: A Status Report,* Congressional Research Service. Washington, D.C.: Library of Congress. 1991.

Schobel, Bruce D. "Sooner Than You Think: The Coming Bankruptcy of Social Security". *Policy Review* (The Heritage Foundation, Washington, D.C.) 62 (Fall 1992):41.

Schulder, Daniel J. Statement by the National Council of Senior Citizens before the 1994–1995 Advisory Council on Social Security. Washington, D.C., March 9, 1995.

Schuller, Tom. *Age, Capital and Democracy.* Burlington, Vt.: Gowen Publishing Company Limited, 1986.

Senate Judiciary Committee, U.S. Congress. Hearings Economic Concentration on 89th Cong. 1st sess., 1965.

Siegel, Alan. *Living Legacy: A History of the Franklin Institute of Boston and the Franklin Foundation.* Ed. Owen Andrews. Boston, 1993.

Shipman, William G. "Retiring With Dignity: Social Security's Harmful Role—Capital Markets' Helpful Solution." Unpublished paper, State Street Bank, Boston, Mass., 1995.

Smith, James, and Calvert Staunton. *Estimating the Wealth of Top Wealth-Holders From Estate Tax Returns.* American Statistical Association. Washington, D.C., 1965.

Social Security Administration. "Male Covered Worker Rates (per Hundred) and Female Covered Worker Rates (per Hundred)." Memorandum to Sam Beard. Data from PROJ2.12. Baltimore, Md., 1995.

Social Security Administration, Office of Research and Statistics. *Annual Statistical Supplement, 1994, to the Social Security Bulletin.* SSA Publication no. 13-11700. Washington, D.C.: U.S. Department of Health and Human Services, August 1994.

——— ."Social Security Programs in the United States." *Social Security Bulletin 56,* no. 4 (Winter 1993).

Soltow, Lee. *Six Papers on the Size Distribution of Wealth and Income.* National Bureau of Economic Research. New York, 1969.

Speiser, Stuart M., ed. *Mainstream Capitalism: Essays on Broadening Share Ownership in America and Britain.* New York: New Horizons Press, 1988.

——— , ed. *Equitable Capitalism: Promoting Economic Opportunity Through Broader Capital Ownership.* New York: Apex Press 1991.

——— . *Ethical Economics & The Faith Community.* Bloomington, Ind.: Meyer Stone Books, 1989.

Steffens, John L. *The "One-Percent Solution": Social Security Reform.* Merrill Lynch Private Client Group. Plainsboro, N.J., August 18, 1994.

Steuerle, C. Eugene, and Jon M. Bakija. *Retooling Social Security for the Twenty-first Century: Right and Wrong Approaches to Reform.* Washington, D.C.: Urban Institute Press, 1994.

Teachers Insurance and Annuity Association College Retirement Equities Fund (TIAA-CREF). *Annual Report 1991.* New York, 1992.

——— . *Estimating Your Retirement Income* Library Series no. 5. New York, 1992.

——— . *This Is TIAA-CREF.* New York, 1992.

——— . *TIAA Investment Supplement 1991.* New York, 1992.

The International Center for Pension Reform. Santiago, Chile: ICPR, n.d.

Tsongas, Paul. *A Call to Economic Arms.* The Tsongas Committee. Boston, 1992.

Turner, John A., and Lorna M. Dailey, eds. *Pension Policy: An International Perspective.* U.S. Department of Labor, Pension and Welfare Benefits Administration. Washington, D.C.: U.S. Government Printing Office, 1991.

U.S. Bureau of Labor Statistics. *Supplement to the Current Population Survey.* Washington, D.C.: U.S. Government Printing Office, January 1991.

Vedder, Richard K., and Lowell E. Gallaway. *Out of Work: Unemployment and Government in Twentieth-Century America.* Oakland, Calif.: Independent Institute, 1994.

Weaver, Carolyn L. *Is Our Public Pension System Beyond Repair?* Washington, D.C.: American Enterprise Institute, August 1994.

——— . Paper presented at Conference on Social Security and Business Costs, sponsored by the Tax Council and IRET, American Enterprise Institute, Washington, D.C., February 9, 1995.

——— . *Social Security Investment Policy: What Is It and How Can It Be Improved.* Washington, D.C.: American Enterprise Institute, August, 1994.

——— . *Social Security Reform after the 1983 Amendments: What Remains to Be Done?* American Enterprise Institute. Washington, D.C., May 1994.

——— , ed. *Social Security's Looming Surpluses: Prospects and Implications.* American Enterprise Institute. Washington, D.C.: AEI Press, 1990.

Williamson, John B., and Eric R. Kingson. "Generational Equity or Privatization of Social Security." *Society* 28, no. 6 (September/October 1991): 38.

Woodruff, Tom. Telephone interview by Sam Beard, November 11, 1994.

About the Author

Sam Beard is chairman of the National Development Council and president of the American Institute for Public Service, which was cofounded by Jacqueline Kennedy Onassis and Senator Robert Taft, Jr. He has worked in economic revitalization in America for twenty-seven years, having found his interest in economic opportunity and social change as a young staff associate in the Senate office of Robert Kennedy.

Beard has founded and chaired economic development programs for presidents Nixon, Ford, Carter, and Reagan. Each of these programs involved investment of more than $1 billion in job creation and economic renewal. He has crafted ground-level development plans on the streets of Bedford-Stuyvesant in the 1960s and has worked over the years with the mayors of more than 100 cities and the governors of more than thirty-five states. His National Development Council programs have resulted in more than $25 billion of private sector investment in poor urban and rural communities and have created more than 500,000 private sector jobs. The author's career-long interest in promoting equal economic opportunity has culminated in the bold—and workable— expansion of capital ownership proposed in this book.

Beard is a graduate of Yale University. Married and the father of three children, he lives in Wilmington, Delaware.

"Tackles the tough issue of how to protect current beneficiaries and at the same time ensure dignity in retirement for future generations. Everyone should read *Restoring Hope in America* and get involved in the debate about Social Security." **Dorcas Hardy**
Former U.S. commissioner of Social Security

"Sam Beard documents in detail the problems facing America's Social Security system. . . . policymakers need to begin working today to reform Social Security in order to prevent a potential political and economic catastrophe down the road." **Paul Beckner**
President, Citizens for a Sound Economy

"Sam Beard, a liberal community-development activist, has seen firsthand that capitalism requires capital. His thought-provoking plan for renewing America's thrift ethic, expanding economic opportunity, and saving Social Security deserves serious attention." **Paul S. Hewitt**
Executive director, National Taxpayers Union Foundation